For

History

Book of Unusual Knowledge

Ben Wilder

HARDCOVER ISBN: **978-969-5492-91-8**

PAPERBACK ISBN: 978-969-5492-90-1

Made in the USA

EXCLUSIVE BONUS

Scan This Code to GET FREE DIGITAL COPIES of
1147 random and Interesting FUN Facts
1000+ Interesting and Mind-Blowing Facts For Curious Minds

Table of Contents

Introduction

History, as you know it, is a lie. A carefully constructed narrative, woven from half-truths and outright deceptions, designed to keep you in the dark. The truth, the *real* history of humanity, has been buried, suppressed, and hidden away in dusty archives and forbidden texts. But now, the time has come to unveil the secrets that have been kept from you for far too long.

In your hands, you hold the key to unlocking the forbidden. This book, "***Forbidden History: History that is not allowed and will blow your mind***", is not just another rehashing of tired old stories. It's a bombshell, a revelation, a journey into the heart of the unknown. Prepare to have your mind blown wide open as we explore the deepest, darkest corners of our past, exposing the shocking truths that have been deliberately concealed.

Do you know about human evolution? Think again. We'll explore the inexplicable leaps in human development, the evidence of advanced prehistoric technologies, and the tantalizing possibility that we are not alone in the universe. We'll journey to ancient Egypt, Sumeria, and the Americas, where enigmatic civilizations arose with knowledge and technologies that defy explanation.

But why has this history been forbidden? Who benefits from keeping us in ignorance? We'll shine a light on the shadowy forces that have worked tirelessly to suppress the truth – secret societies, the Vatican's hidden archives, and the lost libraries of the ancient world. We'll expose the systematic suppression of scientific discoveries that threaten the status quo, and the untold stories of the World Wars that could rewrite our understanding of the 20th century.

Hold on tight as we venture into the realm of the unexplained and the paranormal. We'll investigate UFO sightings, extraterrestrial intervention, and the mysteries of Atlantis and Lemuria. We'll unlock the secrets of the pyramids, explore the power of the mind, and peer into the future of forbidden history itself.

This is not for the faint of heart. This book challenges everything you thought you knew, shattering the comfortable illusions of mainstream history. It's a call to awaken, to question, to seek the truth that has been hidden in plain sight.

But be warned: once you step through the looking glass, there's no going back. The world will never look the same again.

Why This Book is Different

This isn't just speculation or conspiracy theory. Every claim in this book is backed by scientific evidence, images, and illustrations that have been deliberately suppressed, ignored, or dismissed by those who seek to control the narrative. We'll present the evidence, analyze it critically, and let you draw your conclusions.

You'll see ancient artifacts that defy explanation, texts that speak of lost civilizations and advanced technologies, and images that hint at contact with beings from other worlds. You'll learn about the scientists, researchers, and archaeologists who have dared to challenge the official story, often at great personal cost.

This book is their vindication. It's a testament to the courage of those who have sought the truth, no matter the consequences. And it's an invitation for you to join the ranks of the truth-seekers, to become part of a growing movement that is reclaiming our hidden history.

Are You Ready for the Truth?

If you're tired of the lies and distortions of mainstream history, if you're ready to face the truth, no matter how shocking or unsettling, then this book is for you. It's time to break free from the shackles of ignorance and embrace the forbidden.

The journey begins now.

Part I: The Untold Story of Humanity's Origins

The conventional narrative surrounding humanity's origins has remained largely unchallenged in academic circles for decades. The story of evolution, rooted in Darwinian principles, asserts that life is the result of gradual changes wrought by natural selection acting on random mutations. This theory, while revolutionary in its time, is now showing signs of considerable strain. We must reevaluate the foundational premises of Darwinism, especially in light of emerging scientific evidence that contradicts long-held beliefs about the lineage of humanity.

Charles Darwin's theory of evolution has long been viewed as an infallible pillar of modern science, but a closer examination reveals cracks in its foundation that threaten to unravel the entire structure. This part will dissect the inadequacies and contradictions inherent in Darwinian evolution, illustrating how the quest for missing links between species has become a futile endeavor. As we navigate through historical context and contemporary research, we will unveil a narrative that challenges the established paradigms of human origins.

Darwin's original premise, introduced in *The Origin of Species* (1859), was groundbreaking yet simplistic. He postulated that all life on Earth has evolved through a series of random genetic mutations and natural selection. The oft-cited "survival of the fittest" became the cornerstone of this theory. Yet, as the 20th century progressed, the cracks began to widen.

In his correspondence, Darwin himself expressed concern over the "abominable mystery" of flowering plants' origins, acknowledging that gaps in the fossil record could undermine his theories. Despite over a century of scientific inquiry, the search for transitional fossils—those that would bridge the gap between species—has largely yielded silence. Renowned paleontologist Stephen Jay Gould, hardly a proponent of creationism, bluntly stated, “All paleontologists know that the fossil record contains precious little in the way of intermediate forms.” This sentiment encapsulates a critical failure in Darwinism: the absence of evidence to substantiate its core tenets.

The quest for transitional species has become a Sisyphean task. Researchers, excavators, and amateur fossil hunters have combed through the Earth's strata for remnants of our evolutionary past, yet significant findings that could validate Darwin’s model remain elusive. The fossils we do uncover often belong to distinct species, providing no clear evidence of the gradual transformation from one to another. The much-hyped Java Man and Piltdown Man, once heralded as the missing links, were later exposed as either misclassified or outright frauds, undermining the credibility of those advocating for a linear descent from apes to humans.

Michael Behe, a biochemist and author of *Darwin's Black Box*, argues that many biological systems are "irreducibly complex." He illustrates his point by examining processes like blood clotting and the human immune system, which he asserts cannot be explained through gradual Darwinian evolution. Behe's arguments are not mere conjectures; they are grounded in a scientific understanding of molecular biology that Darwin could not have foreseen. The discovery of DNA and the complexities of cellular mechanisms expose the inadequacies of Darwin's model in accounting for the intricacies of life.

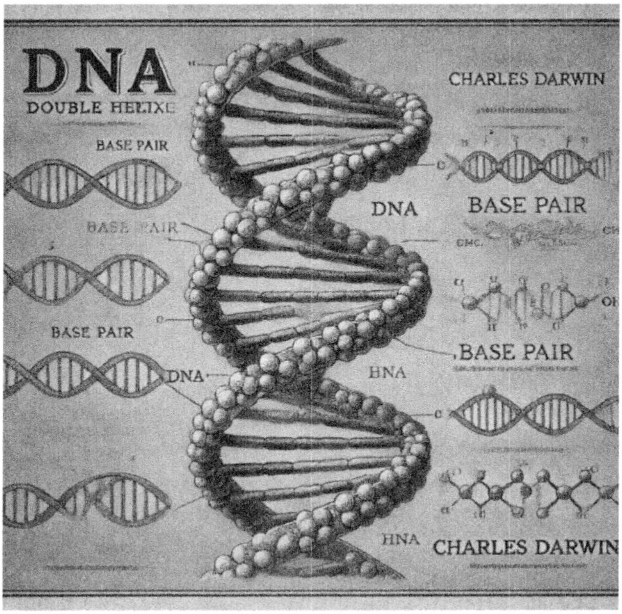

This image shows a DNA structure symbolizing the complexity that challenges Darwinian evolution.

The problems with Darwin's theory do not end with the fossil record or biochemistry. Genetic research indicates that the majority of mutations are either neutral or detrimental. If evolution were predominantly driven by random mutations, we would expect to see a gradual progression of species; instead, the evidence suggests a pattern of stasis and the sudden appearance of new forms—a phenomenon that has led some scientists to propose alternative models like punctuated equilibrium. Gould's theory offers a framework that acknowledges the abrupt shifts in the fossil record while attempting to align them with the broader narrative of Darwinian evolution. However, even this theory does not satisfactorily address the absence of transitional fossils, a fundamental flaw in the evolutionary narrative.

Critics of Darwinism have pointed to these gaps as evidence of a flawed theory that fails to meet the rigorous standards of scientific proof. They question why a theory that claims to describe the very fabric of life has not yielded concrete evidence to support its claims. The reluctance of some in the scientific community to confront these issues publicly is, in part, a reflection of the dogma surrounding Darwinian thought. Fear of professional repercussions stifles dissenting voices, forcing many scientists to toe the line of accepted narratives rather than challenging them.

In this climate of intellectual conformity, there exists a body of evidence that contradicts mainstream views. Richard Milton, a science journalist, has noted that the absence of transitional fossils compelled him to reevaluate the Darwinian framework. His investigations revealed a plethora of anomalous findings that, if accepted, would necessitate a fundamental rethinking of human origins. The prevailing narrative that humans evolved from primitive ancestors is being challenged by evidence suggesting that modern humans existed far earlier than the timeline proposed by standard evolutionary theory.

Evolution vs. Creation: A False Dichotomy?

The debate surrounding human origins is often framed as a binary conflict between evolution and creationism. Yet, this framing obscures a more nuanced conversation that encompasses multiple theories and interpretations of our past. The biblical account of creation, while popular among certain groups, does not align with scientific findings, particularly regarding the age of the Earth and the timeline of human development. However, the rigidity of orthodox creationism contrasts sharply with the flexibility of modern interpretations of intelligent design, which posits that an inherent intelligence underlies the complexities of the universe.

Many scientists and scholars are now suggesting that the creationist versus Darwinian debate may be missing the mark entirely. The works of Richard Thompson and Michael Cremo in *Forbidden Archeology* present a compelling case for the existence of anatomically modern humans long before the accepted timelines. They draw upon evidence of advanced civilizations and sophisticated tools that predate our conventional understanding of human development.

Recent discoveries, including human footprints found alongside dinosaur tracks and stone tools dating back millions of years, challenge the notion that humanity is a recent development. These findings suggest that human beings have existed far longer than previously believed and that our origins may lie within a far more complex narrative than either traditional creationism or Darwinism suggests.

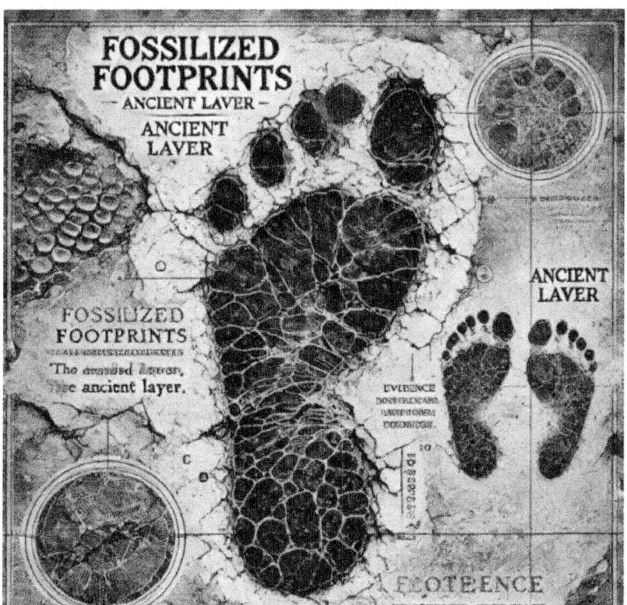

Fossilized footprints surrounding human origin

Moreover, a growing body of evidence supports the idea of catastrophic events shaping the course of evolution, further complicating the traditional gradualist model. Theories of sudden disruptions, such as meteor impacts or drastic climate changes, have gained traction among some scientists. These theories suggest that such catastrophic events could have accelerated evolutionary changes and led to the emergence of new species.

The skepticism towards Darwinism is not merely a religious backlash against science; rather, it reflects a growing recognition of the limitations inherent in the traditional evolutionary framework. As more evidence comes to light, it is essential to remain open to alternative explanations that might account for the complex tapestry of human history.

New Perspectives on Ancient Knowledge

The revelations of ancient civilizations, as proposed by researchers like Graham Hancock and the Flem-Aths, bring to light a rich array of human history that has been overlooked. Their theories suggest the existence of a sophisticated prehistoric civilization that possessed advanced knowledge of astronomy and engineering long before the dawn of recorded history. The idea that humanity may have shared a common cultural heritage, transcending geographical boundaries, opens up a new avenue of exploration in the quest to understand our origins.

Evidence such as ancient maps, which accurately depict coastlines now submerged, points to a society with remarkable navigational capabilities. This challenges the prevailing notion that early humans were simple nomadic hunter-gatherers. The sophistication of megalithic structures in regions like Bolivia and Egypt further supports the argument that a high level of technological expertise existed among ancient peoples, contrary to the simplistic narratives of human evolution.

The prevalence of similar myths and legends across cultures suggests a shared understanding of cosmic events and human origins. The study of etymology reveals deep-rooted connections between languages, hinting at a common ancestral language that transcended time and geography. As we explore these ancient narratives, we begin to understand that the story of humanity is far more intricate than the linear progression proposed by traditional evolution.

In unraveling the riddles of human evolution, we find ourselves standing at a crossroads. The overwhelming evidence suggesting the inadequacies of Darwinian theory forces us to confront uncomfortable truths about our past. As the search for missing links continues to yield silence, the need for a comprehensive understanding of human origins becomes increasingly urgent.

The rigid dichotomy of evolution versus creationism fails to capture the complexity of the evidence at hand. New perspectives and alternative theories are emerging, challenging the status quo and beckoning us to consider the possibility of an intricate, interconnected history of humanity.

As we venture further into the depths of our origins, it is essential to embrace a multidisciplinary approach that combines archaeology, paleontology, genetics, and even ancient wisdom. In doing so, we may finally begin to piece together the enigmatic puzzle of human evolution—a quest that remains both vital and unfinished.

Chapter 1: The Riddles of Human Evolution

The narrative of human evolution is fraught with controversy, ridicule, and, at times, outright suppression. What we believe about our origins is not merely an academic exercise; it shapes our understanding of humanity itself. The story is as much about the evidence we have uncovered as it is about the evidence that has been overlooked, ignored, or actively concealed. The time has come to confront the riddles of human evolution head-on, armed with the power of inquiry and the audacity to question the narratives we've been fed.

The Emergence of Darwinian Thought

On a notable evening in 1871, the Red Lions—a circle of learned gentlemen in Edinburgh—gathered to celebrate knowledge through laughter and song. Among the highlights was Lord Neaves, whose witty lyrics about Charles Darwin's groundbreaking work, *The Origin of Species*, humorously acknowledged the implications of Darwin's theories: "An Ape with a pliable thumb and big brain, / when the gift of gab he had managed to gain, / As Lord of Creation established his reign / Which Nobody can Deny!" This lighthearted moment belied the serious contention brewing around the question of human origins. Just a decade after Darwin's landmark publication, the scientific community was beginning to grapple with the unsettling notion that humans might not occupy a privileged position in the hierarchy of life.

In *The Origin of Species*, Darwin carefully skirted the topic of human evolution, only hinting that our origins would eventually be clarified. However, it was in his 1871 work, *Descent of Man*, that he boldly asserted humanity's connection to a lineage of apelike ancestors. His proclamation that "man is descended from a hairy, tailed quadruped" shocked many and ignited fierce debates within scientific and public circles. This foundational assertion was, however, made with a glaring absence of transitional fossil evidence, a point that Darwin himself recognized as a potential vulnerability in his argument.

The Fossil Record: A Double-Edged Sword

The fossil record, or the lack thereof, has often been used as a weapon against Darwin's theory. Critics clamored for tangible proof of the evolutionary pathway that linked humans to their primate ancestors. At the time, only two Neanderthal skulls, along with scant fossil evidence, were available to support claims of human evolution. This dearth of evidence became fodder for those who refused to accept the implications of Darwinian theory. Critics demanded to see the fossilized remains that would substantiate Darwin's claims—where were the "missing links"?

Fast forward to today, and the landscape of paleoanthropology has transformed dramatically. A wealth of fossil evidence has emerged from Africa, Asia, and beyond, providing clearer insights into human ancestry. The first hominids—erect-walking humanlike primates—are thought to have appeared during the Pliocene epoch, with *Australopithecus* marking a pivotal step in our evolutionary journey. Standing between 4 and 5 feet tall, with a cranial capacity of 300 to 600 cubic centimeters (cc), this early ancestor shared a peculiar mix of human and apelike features.

One branch of *Australopithecus* is believed to have given rise to *Homo habilis* approximately 2 million years ago, heralding the onset of the Pleistocene. Here, we see a gradual increase in cranial capacity, indicating a potential for greater cognitive abilities. This pattern continues with *Homo erectus*, the species that included Java man and Beijing man, which arose around 1.5 million years ago, standing between 5 and 6 feet tall with a cranial capacity ranging from 700 to 1,300 cc. Yet, the characteristics of *Homo erectus*—massive brow ridges and a sloping forehead—still reflect a connection to earlier hominids.

A Timeline of Human Ancestry

Paleoanthropologists currently posit that anatomically modern humans, or *Homo sapiens sapiens*, emerged from *Homo erectus* around 300,000 to 400,000 years ago. However, the narrative becomes complicated as evidence suggests that both modern humans and Neanderthals may have evolved from earlier hominids, specifically pre-Neanderthal types of *Homo sapiens*. The struggle for identity in our evolutionary past continues to raise challenging questions about our lineage and the broader implications for human history.

The picture grows murkier when we consider the evidence for Neanderthals. Once deemed direct ancestors of modern humans, their classification has since been debated. Despite having larger brains than *Homo sapiens sapiens*, their evolutionary lineage appears distinct, complicating the tidy narrative of human evolution that many have come to accept. As we peel back the layers of this study, we are compelled to confront the underlying assumptions that have driven our understanding of human origins.

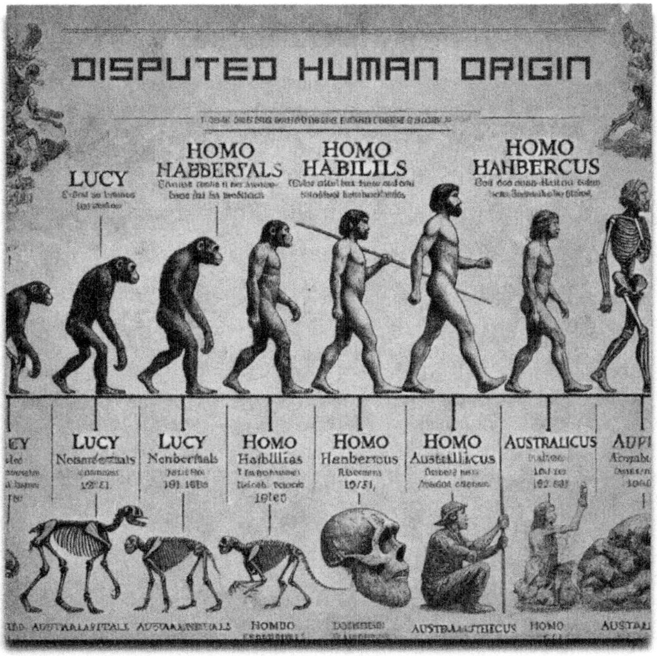

Timeline illustrating disputed human origins and early hominid fossils

The Gaps in the Record

Despite the advancements in paleoanthropological research, significant gaps remain in our understanding of human descent. Notably, there exists a void of fossil evidence bridging the gap between Miocene apes and the Pliocene ancestors of modern humans. The prevailing scientific consensus has largely accepted a narrative of gradual evolution, yet what if future discoveries challenge this framework?

There are tantalizing hints of findings that contradict established timelines. In the late nineteenth and early twentieth centuries, various discoveries suggested the presence of anatomically modern humans much earlier than previously thought. Reports of human skeletal remains and sophisticated tools have surfaced in geological layers dated far older than the accepted timeline of human habitation.

Consider the case of *Hueyatlaco* in Mexico, where archaeologist Virginia Steen-McIntyre's team found tools that dated back 250,000 years, significantly older than the mainstream acceptance of human arrival in the Americas. Instead of igniting a scientific revolution, Steen-McIntyre faced vilification and professional ruin. Her findings were disregarded and dismissed as anomalies that could not possibly fit within the established timeline of human evolution.

Similarly, California state geologist J.D. Whitney authenticated numerous stone artifacts and human fossils unearthed from geological strata dating between nine to fifty-five million years old. The implications were profound, yet these findings vanished from scholarly discourse, eclipsed by a scientific community reluctant to confront evidence that challenged the prevailing paradigm.

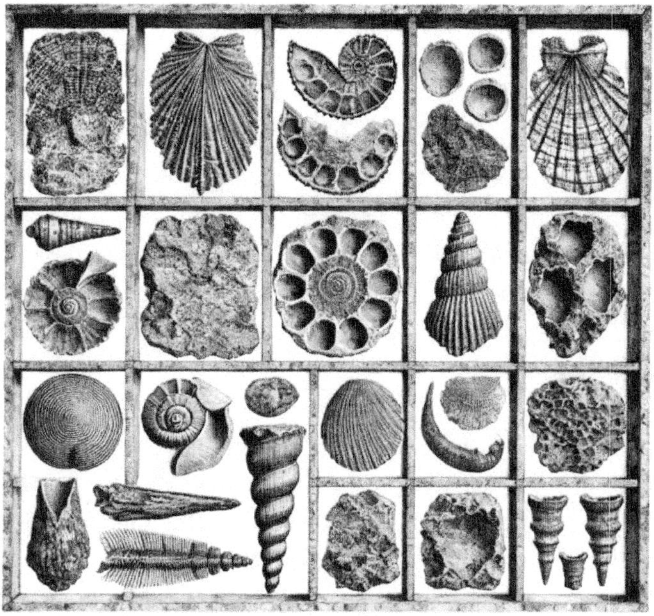
Artifacts From Ancient Geological Strata

Suppressed Evidence and the Politics of Knowledge

This brings us to the crux of the matter: the politics of knowledge and the suppression of evidence. Scholars like Michael Cremo and Richard Thompson, in their controversial work *Forbidden Archeology*, have exposed a systematic tendency within the scientific community to ignore or discredit findings that contradict established theories. They argue that this behavior reflects not merely scientific caution, but an entrenched academic elitism more concerned with maintaining its authority than seeking the truth.

Cremo's investigations reveal a landscape littered with ignored discoveries and suppressed evidence. For instance, in South Africa, miners have been retrieving small metallic spheres from strata nearly three billion years old. Yet, the scientific community has largely failed to acknowledge these artifacts, effectively maintaining a narrative that human history is far shorter and less complex than it may be.

The fabric of scientific inquiry has been marred by instances of professional misconduct, whether through neglect or outright fraud. The infamous Piltdown Man hoax stands as a testament to the potential for deception within the field. As we dissect these narratives, we uncover a web of motivations: the drive for prestige, the fear of ridicule, and the desire to uphold a cherished worldview.

Epistemology and the Limits of Knowledge

Before delving deeper into the labyrinth of human evolution, it is essential to outline some principles of epistemology—the study of knowledge and its limits. The limitations inherent in paleoanthropological research are significant. Discoveries in this field are often rare and cannot be replicated easily. Many prominent scientists have built their reputations on a handful of finds, while others labor in obscurity.

Moreover, the act of excavation itself destroys crucial context. Once a fossil is removed from its strata, the direct evidence of its position is lost, and knowledge relies solely on the excavator's testimony. The complexities of geological formations can further obscure the significance of discoveries, leading to discrepancies among observers.

The potential for fraud—whether deliberate or inadvertent—also looms large in this field. If the scientific community clings too tightly to established narratives, it risks overlooking critical evidence simply because it does not align with prevailing theories. The natural human tendency to reject findings that contradict one’s beliefs can inhibit the pursuit of truth, leading to a collective amnesia about our past.

Re-evaluating the Evidence

In examining the various claims surrounding human origins, we must adopt a comparative approach. By evaluating the quality of different reports and considering the context of their discoveries, we can gain insights that may not be readily apparent. Just because the evidence does not fit neatly into our existing framework does not mean it lacks validity. To dismiss it outright is to undermine the scientific process itself.

If we accept the existence of anomalous artifacts and human skeletal remains dating back much further than the mainstream narrative allows, we must grapple with the implications for our understanding of human history. Such discoveries could suggest the presence of intelligent, tool-making beings in geological periods previously thought uninhabited by humans.

This does not merely challenge the modern theory of human evolution; it prompts a radical rethinking of our entire understanding of mammalian life during the Cenozoic era. If anatomically modern humans existed alongside earlier hominids, we must confront uncomfortable truths about our identity and our history.

The Resistance to New Ideas

The response of the scientific establishment to challenges posed by alternative theories has often been one of hostility. Individuals who dare to question the status quo, like Steen-McIntyre, have found their careers derailed. This phenomenon is not an isolated incident; it is indicative of a broader trend where scientific orthodoxy prioritizes its survival over genuine inquiry.

Cremo's observations regarding the Rockefeller Foundation's involvement in funding research reveal a more insidious layer of control over the narrative of human origins. The motivations behind the funding of research projects can have profound implications for the direction of scientific inquiry. When those in power dictate the agenda, the potential for knowledge to flourish diminishes significantly.

The implications of these findings extend beyond mere academic curiosity. They touch on our understanding of ourselves and our place in the universe. If we are willing to entertain the notion that our origins are more complex than we have been led to believe, we open the door to a host of questions that challenge our fundamental beliefs.

The riddles of human evolution demand our attention. It is time to challenge the narratives we have accepted without question and to scrutinize the evidence that has been marginalized or suppressed. The history of human origins is a dynamic and contentious field, one that requires us to approach it with skepticism and curiosity.

This chapter serves as an invitation to explore the complexities and contradictions inherent in the story of our evolution. Let us embrace the uncertainties and seek the truth, regardless of where it leads. The quest for understanding our past is not merely an academic endeavor; it is a vital exploration of what it means to be human.

As we move forward in this book, let us remain vigilant in our examination of history, unearthing the suppressed narratives and forgotten truths that lie beneath the surface of conventional thought. Only then can we hope to unravel the profound mysteries of human evolution.

Chapter 2: Unveiling Java Man—The Controversial Keystone in Human Evolution

In the late nineteenth century, a significant faction within the scientific community was coalescing around a groundbreaking idea: that anatomically modern humans might have existed far earlier than previously thought, possibly extending back into the Pliocene and Miocene epochs—or even earlier. This notion challenged the prevailing paradigms of human evolution and threatened to upend established timelines.

One of the most prominent figures to embrace this radical perspective was Alfred Russel Wallace, a contemporary of Charles Darwin and co-discoverer of the theory of evolution by natural selection. Wallace's willingness to entertain the idea of ancient modern humans put him at odds with Darwin, who viewed such notions as heretical and damaging to the credibility of evolutionary theory. The tension between these intellectual giants highlighted the contentious atmosphere surrounding human origins at the time.

However, the discovery that would dramatically shift the discourse was imminent. News began to circulate about the unearthing of remarkable fossilized remains on the island of Java, which seemed to bridge the gap between apes and humans. This finding, later known as Java Man, would not only challenge existing theories but also play a pivotal role in discrediting earlier evidence suggesting the great antiquity of modern humans. To fully grasp the impact of this discovery, we must delve into its history and the controversies it ignited.

Eugene Dubois and the Quest for the Missing Link

The story begins with Eugene Dubois, a Dutch anatomist and physician born in 1858—the year before Darwin published "On the Origin of Species." Despite being raised in a devout Catholic family, Dubois was captivated by the concept of evolution, particularly its implications for human ancestry. He recognized a critical gap in Darwin's theory: the lack of fossil evidence documenting the transition from apes to humans.

Determined to find the elusive "missing link," Dubois meticulously studied the skeletal remains of Neanderthals, which were among the few hominid fossils known at the time. However, these specimens were too similar to modern humans to represent a true transitional form. Influenced by the German biologist Ernst Haeckel, who had predicted the discovery of an intermediate species he named Pithecanthropus (from the Greek words for "ape" and "man"), Dubois resolved to unearth this creature himself.

Convinced that the tropics of Africa or Southeast Asia would yield the desired fossils, Dubois set his sights on the Dutch East Indies (present-day Indonesia), where he could leverage his nationality to gain access. Unable to secure funding for a dedicated scientific expedition, he enlisted as an army surgeon and departed for Sumatra with his wife in December 1887, sacrificing a comfortable academic position for the uncertainties of the unknown.

In Sumatra, Dubois scoured limestone caves, uncovering animal fossils and remnants of early humans but nothing that fit the profile of the ape-man he sought. A bout of malaria in 1890 prompted his transfer to Java, offering new opportunities for exploration. Settling near the Solo River, he began excavations that would soon yield extraordinary results.

The Discovery at Trinil

In 1891, Dubois's laborers unearthed a fossilized molar that appeared to belong to a primate. Initially thinking it was from a giant chimpanzee, Dubois intensified his efforts in the area.

Shortly thereafter, they uncovered a skullcap characterized by a pronounced brow ridge, a feature suggestive of an ape. Although the initial reports did not claim the discovery of a transitional species, Dubois's perception evolved as he analyzed the findings.

The following year, about 15 meters from where the skullcap was found, his team discovered a human-like femur. Another molar surfaced nearby, and Dubois began to entertain the idea that these remains might belong to the same individual—a creature that exhibited both ape-like and human-like characteristics. He named it Pithecanthropus erectus, or "erect ape-man," positing that it represented a true intermediary between apes and humans.

Dubois based his assertion on several factors. The cranial capacity of the skull was estimated to be between 800 and 1,000 cubic centimeters—larger than that of modern apes but smaller than that of humans. This, he argued, placed the creature squarely between the two. Additionally, the femur resembled that of modern humans, suggesting bipedal locomotion.

However, critical details cast doubt on Dubois's conclusions. The skullcap and femur were found at a considerable distance from each other in a site rich with various animal fossils. The possibility that the bones belonged to different species was significant, yet Dubois maintained they were from a single individual.

Reception and Controversy

When Dubois presented his findings to the scientific community in Europe, reactions were mixed. Evolutionary proponents like Haeckel hailed the discovery as the long-sought missing link, while skeptics questioned the association of the skullcap and femur, the interpretation of the cranial capacity, and the overall validity of the claim.

Virchow, a prominent pathologist, dismissed the skullcap as that of a giant gibbon and asserted that the femur was unequivocally human. He argued that no evidence connected the two bones to the same organism. This skepticism underscored a broader debate within the scientific community about the interpretation of fossil evidence and the construction of human evolutionary history.

Despite the controversy, Java Man gained traction as a key piece of evidence for human evolution. It served as a counterargument to claims that modern humans had existed unchanged for millions of years—a notion that threatened the foundations of evolutionary theory.

The Selenka Expedition and Further Doubts

To address lingering questions, the Selenka Expedition was organized in 1907-1908, led by Professor Lenore Selenka after her husband's death. The team conducted extensive excavations at Trinil but failed to find additional Pithecanthropus fossils. Instead, they uncovered artifacts suggesting the presence of modern humans, including stone tools and hearths.

These findings implied that anatomically modern humans might have coexisted with Pithecanthropus erectus, challenging the linear progression implied by Dubois's interpretation. Moreover, a human molar found in older strata than those containing Pithecanthropus further complicated the narrative.

Dubois's Retreat and the Emergence of Homo Erectus

Faced with mounting skepticism, Dubois became increasingly reclusive, withdrawing his fossils from public view for decades. During this period, the scientific community grappled with the implications of his discovery. Some researchers proposed that the skullcap and femur did not belong together, and debates about the interpretation of the fossils persisted.

Meanwhile, discoveries in Africa and China introduced additional hominid species into the evolutionary framework. The concept of Homo erectus emerged, encompassing both Java Man and Peking Man, discovered in the Zhoukoudian cave near Beijing in the 1920s. These fossils exhibited a mix of primitive and advanced features, reinforcing the idea of a transitional species between apes and modern humans.

Revisiting the Femur Controversy

In the 1970s, researchers reexamined the femurs associated with Java Man. Studies revealed that these femurs were anatomically modern, differing from those of Homo erectus specimens found elsewhere. This raised the possibility that anatomically modern humans had existed alongside Homo erectus in Java approximately 800,000 years ago—a notion that conflicted with established timelines.

Some scientists suggested that the femurs might have been mixed into older deposits from higher strata, but this explanation was speculative. The association between the femurs and the skullcap remained dubious, and the integrity of the original findings was further called into question.

The Piltdown Man Debacle

Amid the ongoing debates surrounding Java Man, another sensational discovery shook the scientific world: Piltdown Man. Unearthed in England between 1908 and 1911, the Piltdown fossils consisted of a human-like skull and an ape-like jaw, seemingly providing the perfect transitional form.

For decades, Piltdown Man was celebrated as a crucial piece of evidence for human evolution. However, in the 1950s, advanced testing methods revealed that the fossils were a forgery—a modern human skull combined with an orangutan jaw, artificially aged to deceive researchers.

The Piltdown hoax had a profound impact on the field of paleoanthropology. It highlighted the susceptibility of scientists to confirmation bias and the dangers of accepting evidence that neatly fits preconceived theories without rigorous scrutiny. The scandal also cast a shadow over other discoveries, including Java Man, prompting a reevaluation of the evidence.

Reassessing Java Man's Place in Human Evolution

The controversies surrounding both Java Man and Piltdown Man underscored the complexities of reconstructing human evolutionary history. As new fossils were discovered and analytical techniques advanced, the narrative continued to evolve.

Modern consensus places Homo erectus as a legitimate ancestor of Homo sapiens, with Java Man representing one regional variant. Yet, questions remain about the coexistence of anatomically modern humans and Homo erectus, as suggested by the femur findings in Java.

These ambiguities point to a more intricate picture of human evolution than a straightforward linear progression. The possibility of multiple hominid species cohabiting and potentially interbreeding complicates the traditional models and calls for a more nuanced understanding.

The Role of Scientific Institutions and Funding

The pursuit of human origins has always been intertwined with broader philosophical and societal implications. Institutions like the Carnegie Institution and the Rockefeller Foundation played significant roles in funding research expeditions, including those led by Dubois and later by Gustav von Koenigswald in Java.

John C. Merriam, president of the Carnegie Institution, saw the study of human evolution as pivotal to shaping modern philosophy and belief systems. By strategically allocating resources to support specific lines of inquiry, these institutions influenced the direction of scientific research and, consequently, the narratives constructed about human ancestry.

Later Discoveries and Ongoing Debates

Subsequent excavations in Java and elsewhere continued to yield hominid fossils. Many of these finds were surface discoveries made by local collectors, raising concerns about their stratigraphic context and accurate dating. The reliance on artifacts obtained under such conditions introduced uncertainties that complicated the interpretation of the fossil record.

Chemical and radiometric dating methods, including potassium-argon dating and fluorine analysis, provided age estimates for the fossil-bearing strata. However, inconsistencies and limitations in these techniques sometimes led to conflicting results. For instance, some dates suggested that Homo erectus existed in Java earlier than in Africa, challenging the "Out of Africa" hypothesis.

Moreover, the possibility that certain fossils attributed to Homo erectus might instead belong to anatomically modern humans—or even to species like Australopithecus—added layers of complexity to the evolutionary timeline.

Misrepresentation and Bias in Paleoanthropology

The history of Java Man reveals not only the scientific challenges inherent in studying ancient hominids but also the influence of cognitive biases and theoretical commitments. Researchers have sometimes selectively presented evidence to support prevailing theories, downplaying or dismissing anomalies that don't fit the expected pattern.

This tendency highlights a broader issue within the scientific community: the filtration of knowledge according to entrenched paradigms. Such practices can hinder the objective evaluation of data and impede the development of more accurate models of human evolution.

The saga of Java Man exemplifies the intricate and often contentious nature of paleoanthropological research. It illustrates how discoveries can both illuminate and obscure our understanding of human origins, depending on how they are interpreted and integrated into existing frameworks.

The debates sparked by Java Man and contemporaneous findings like Piltdown Man underscore the necessity for critical scrutiny, transparency, and openness to revising established narratives in light of new evidence. As our methods and technologies advance, so too must our willingness to challenge assumptions and embrace the complexities of our ancestral past.

The quest to unravel the story of human evolution is far from over. Each discovery has the potential to reshape our understanding, reminding us that the journey from our ancient origins to the present is not a straight line but a web of interwoven paths, some of which remain hidden in the depths of time.

Chapter 3: The Forbidden History of Animals

The history of human evolution is often painted with broad strokes, colored by the prevailing theories of the time and the evidence that conveniently fits those narratives. However, the history that remains largely unexplored, buried beneath layers of geological time, suggests a far more complex relationship between humans and the animal kingdom. This chapter delves into the **forbidden history of animals**, focusing on intentionally cut and broken bones, which may be one of the most compelling pieces of evidence for human antiquity.

Unearthing the Evidence: A Historical Perspective

The study of intentionally cut and broken animal bones provides a crucial window into our past. These artifacts emerged as significant evidence for human existence during epochs previously thought to be devoid of modern human life. The initial inquiry into this evidence took shape in the mid-19th century, coinciding with the publication of Charles Darwin's *The Origin of Species*. This groundbreaking work ignited a wave of scientific exploration, leading many to scrutinize fossil records that hinted at early human activity. These discoveries presented a compelling narrative of our prehistoric ancestors who may have coexisted with now-extinct species, prompting a reevaluation of human evolution.

The incised and broken bones found in various locations—particularly from the Pliocene and Miocene epochs—have undergone rigorous examination. Detractors have often attributed the markings to natural causes, such as carnivore activity or geological processes, while proponents of human agency provided counterarguments grounded in experimental archaeology. For instance, they demonstrated that stone tools, akin to those discovered alongside these fossilized bones, could replicate the cut marks observed in the fossil record, establishing a direct link between early humans and their utilization of animal remains.

The St. Prest Controversy

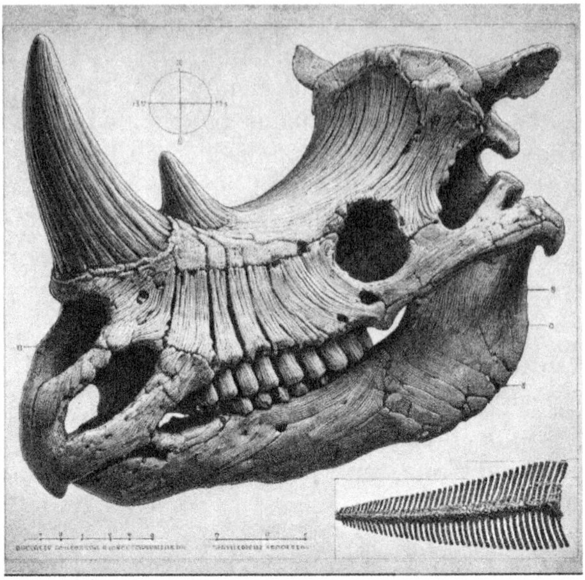

Fossilized rhinoceroses' bone displays prominent incised markings that suggest possible interaction with early humans.

The fossils in question, which include bones of animals like elephants, rhinoceroses, and horses, were first uncovered in the 19th century near the village of Saint-Prest, close to Chartres in France. Initially, some researchers, particularly French paleontologist Jules Desnoyers, suggested that the bones bore marks indicating they had been manipulated by humans. If this interpretation were accurate, it would imply that early humans or human-like ancestors were present in Europe millions of years ago—far earlier than mainstream science currently accepts for the presence of hominids in Europe.

Key Points of the Controversy

1. **Age of the Fossils**: The fossils from St. Prest have been dated to the Miocene or Pliocene epoch, possibly around 2–10 million years ago. This predates the generally accepted time frame for the appearance of Homo species and their ancestors in Europe, based on other fossil evidence and genetic data.
2. **Interpretation of Marks**: Proponents of the idea that these bones were modified by humans argue that the marks resemble tool cuts, which could suggest that ancient humans or their ancestors butchered these animals. Skeptics, however, argue that these marks could have resulted from natural processes such as trampling, sediment pressure, or water erosion rather than human activity.
3. **Scientific Skepticism and Debate**: Over the years, the claims regarding St. Prest have largely been dismissed by the mainstream scientific community, primarily due to the lack of corroborating evidence of human presence in Europe at that time. The absence of stone tools or hominid fossils from the same strata has made it difficult to support the hypothesis that the marks on the animal bones were made by humans.
4. **Impact on Theories of Human Origins**: The St. Prest findings, if verified, would challenge the established timeline of human evolution and migration. Current understanding places the earliest hominins, such as *Sahelanthropus*, *Orrorin*, and *Ardipithecus*, in Africa several million years ago. The generally accepted narrative suggests that hominids did not leave Africa until around 1.8 million years ago, with *Homo erectus*. The St. Prest claims would imply a much earlier spread of hominids into Europe, which lacks corroborating evidence from other archaeological sites.
5. **Continued Interest**: Despite being largely discredited, the St. Prest Controversy continues to capture the imagination of some alternative historians and paleoanthropologists who challenge conventional views on human evolution. It is often cited by proponents of

"forbidden archaeology," a field that posits alternative theories of human history and evolution.

Current Consensus

The current scientific consensus is that the marks on the bones from St. Prest were likely caused by natural processes rather than by human tools. Without additional evidence, such as fossilized human remains or definitive stone tools from the same layers, the claims remain unsubstantiated. However, the controversy underscores the complexities and challenges in interpreting ancient fossils and understanding the deep history of human evolution.

The St. Prest Controversy remains a historical example of how interpretations in archaeology and paleoanthropology can be contentious, especially when findings challenge established timelines or theories.

One pivotal site in this debate is St. Prest, France, where Jules Desnoyers first reported findings of incised rhinoceros bones in 1863. His discovery of narrow grooves and circular marks on the tibia of the rhinoceros raised questions about the potential human influence on these specimens. If indeed these marks were produced by stone tools, as Desnoyers suggested, it could imply that humans inhabited Europe during the Late Pliocene—a notion that directly contradicts the established timeline of human evolution.

This evidence did not go unchallenged. Critics like Gabriel de Mortillet argued that the marks were geological in origin, yet Desnoyers countered with convincing observations about the mineral deposits found on the incisions, which were indistinguishable from those on the surrounding bone. Despite the controversy, the implications of Desnoyers' findings are profound: they suggest a complexity in the human timeline that challenges conventional paleoanthropological narratives.

The persistent dismissal of these findings from contemporary scientific literature raises critical questions about bias in the field. Are we witnessing a refusal to entertain evidence that contradicts long-held beliefs about human evolution? Or is the omission a result of genuine scientific skepticism? Armand de Quatrefages articulated this dilemma, stating that many objections to early human existence in the Pliocene and Miocene seemed rooted in theoretical rather than empirical grounds.

Modern Discoveries: The Old Crow River Case

Fast-forwarding to modern archaeology, the debate continues with discoveries like those at Old Crow River, Canada. In the 1970s, Richard Morlan's investigations into modified bones unearthed evidence suggesting human activity dating back 80,000 years—far older than the traditional narrative of human migration into North America. The meticulous examination of these bones revealed what appeared to be intentional modifications consistent with butchering practices.

However, subsequent studies introduced skepticism regarding the origins of the markings, attributing some to natural processes such as river ice. Morlan's retraction of parts of his earlier claims, while still asserting the authenticity of a few specimens, illustrates the ongoing struggle within paleoanthropology to establish clear evidence of early human presence.

The Anza-Borrego Desert Findings

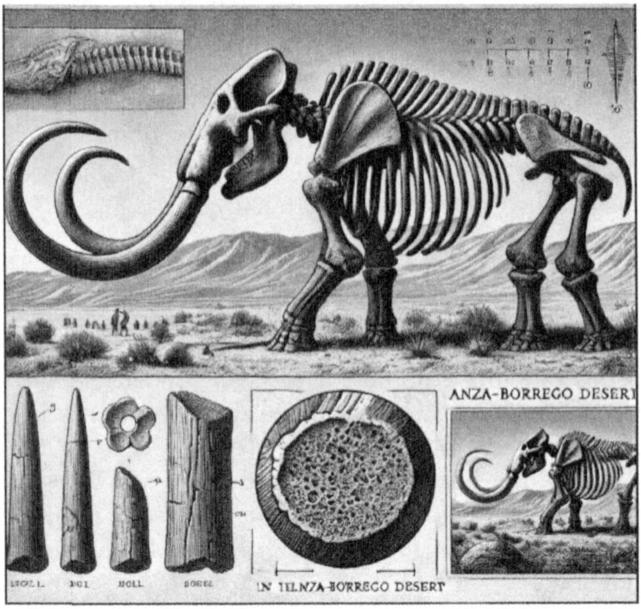

Mammoth bones found in the Anza-Borrego Desert, highlighting incisions that suggest early human activity.

In California's Anza-Borrego Desert, another significant discovery surfaced with the excavation of mammoth bones exhibiting incisions indicative of human activity. George Miller's claims of scratches resembling those made by stone tools suggested that these bones dated back at least 300,000 years. Skepticism from the scientific community, however, overshadowed Miller's assertions, raising questions about the reliability of the excavation process and the absence of accompanying stone tools.

Despite these challenges, the continuity of evidence across diverse sites remains compelling. The similarity of findings in St. Prest, Old Crow River, and Anza-Borrego underscores a potential pattern of ancient human behavior that demands acknowledgment. The consistent nature of these markings across various geographic locations suggests a complex narrative of human-animal interaction that transcends established timelines.

Incised Bones from Italy

The Italian sites of Val d'Arno and others provide further evidence of this narrative. Bones found in the Arno River valley bore marks consistent with human tool use, leading researchers to date them back to the Pliocene. These findings have met with the same skepticism faced by their counterparts in France, as scientists like de Mortillet reiterated doubts about human involvement, often attributing marks to geological processes or the actions of rodents.

However, the repetitive nature of these discoveries presents a robust argument for the need to reevaluate our understanding of human presence during these epochs. As with St. Prest, the lack of acceptance of these findings within mainstream literature speaks to a broader issue of scientific rigidity that may hinder the exploration of new theories regarding human evolution.

Pikermi, Greece: A Site of Controversy

The Pikermi site in Greece stands as another testament to the contentious nature of human origins. The discovery of numerous bones showing signs of methodical fracturing raised alarms among established paleoanthropologists. The careful breaking of bones for marrow extraction—a behavior linked to early hominins—suggests that humans or proto-humans could have existed in the Miocene. The implications of this finding extend beyond mere chronology; they challenge the very framework within which human evolution has been understood.

The methods employed at Pikermi, including the use of stones for butchering, align with those seen in more recent human behavior, reinforcing the idea that the evolutionary lineage of modern humans is far more complex than previously thought.

Anomalous Findings: The Carved Bone and Shell Discoveries

Further reinforcing this narrative are anomalous findings, such as the carved bone from the Dardanelles and the shell with a human face from the Red Crag in England. These artifacts date back millions of years, far preceding the accepted timeline for complex human activity. The intricate carvings suggest a level of cognitive ability that is thought to have only emerged in the last 40,000 years.

The opposition faced by these findings highlights the challenges researchers encounter when presenting evidence that conflicts with established norms. Critics often resort to skepticism rather than engaging with the data, choosing instead to protect their scientific reputations by adhering to a traditional understanding of human development.

The Ongoing Debate: Revisiting the Evidence

The evidence for human activity alongside extinct species during the Pliocene and earlier epochs is substantial yet often dismissed. As we consider the multitude of studies and findings presented over the past century, it becomes clear that a reevaluation of our understanding of human evolution is necessary. The repeated identification of cut marks and tool use across various geographic locations poses significant challenges to conventional narratives and suggests a far more intricate relationship between early humans and their environment than previously acknowledged.

The Institutional Resistance

The institutional resistance to these findings is palpable. Modern paleoanthropologists often operate within rigid frameworks that dictate what evidence is acceptable and what is not. The fear of undermining established theories often leads to the systematic exclusion of contradictory evidence from scholarly discussions. As Armand de Quatrefages noted in the late 19th century, objections to the existence of humans in earlier epochs are frequently based on theoretical considerations rather than empirical evidence. This underscores a significant issue within the scientific community: a reluctance to entertain data that challenges prevailing paradigms.

Deliberately Modified Bones

The growing body of evidence supporting the presence of humans in prehistoric contexts cannot be ignored. From **St. Prest** in France to the **Old Crow River** in Canada, these discoveries raise questions about the nature of our understanding of human evolution. Are we deliberately overlooking data that contradicts established theories, or are we genuinely misunderstanding the complexities of early human life?

The answers to these questions may be less about the findings themselves and more about the frameworks within which we interpret them. As we continue to uncover more evidence from the past, we must challenge the conventional narratives that dominate our understanding of human history. The evidence suggests a deeper connection between humans and the animal kingdom, one that has been obscured by time and the biases of contemporary scholarship.

We stand at a crossroads in our understanding of human history—a moment where the evidence challenges us to reconsider everything we thought we knew about the relationship between humans and the animal kingdom. The study of intentionally modified bones serves not just as an archaeological endeavor but as a call to action for scholars and laypeople alike to dive deeper into the truths of our past, unearthing the stories that have long been suppressed.

Chapter 4: Prehistoric Technologies

The Hueyatlaco Bombshell

The year was 1966. In the sun-drenched heart of Mexico, a team of archaeologists led by Virginia Steen-McIntyre were meticulously excavating two sites, Hueyatlaco and El Horno. They unearthed a large sum of stone tools – some so sophisticated they rivaled the craftsmanship of Cro-Magnon man in Europe. Initial estimates hinted at an age of roughly 20,000 years, placing these artifacts near the supposed dawn of human presence in the Americas. But Steen-McIntyre, a stickler for precision, employed not one, not two, but four independent dating methods to confirm the age of these relics.

Hueyatlaco excavation site

What she uncovered wasn't just a collection of old stones; it was a time bomb ticking away at the foundations of mainstream archaeology. The results screamed an age of 250,000 years – a figure so outlandish it threatened to shatter the established timeline of human history in the New World.

Stone tools from Hueyatlaco

The reaction from the archaeological establishment? Not the rigorous re-evaluation one might expect from a scientific discipline. Instead, Steen-McIntyre faced ridicule, and her career was effectively terminated. The evidence, however, remained – a stark testament to a prehistoric world far more complex than orthodox narratives allowed.

California's Deep-Time Secrets

Fast forward to the gold rush era in California. As miners carved deep into Table Mountain, they inadvertently struck a vein of history far more ancient than any gold nugget.

Hundreds of stone tools and even human fossils emerged from layers of rock dated between 9 and 55 million years old! California's state geologist, J.D. Whitney, meticulously documented these finds, but his reports were met with deafening silence. The implications were simply too radical to stomach, so the evidence was swept under the rug, erased from the textbooks, and forgotten.

South Africa's Billion-Year-Old Enigma

And then we have the curious case of the South African metallic spheres. These perfectly formed objects, etched with parallel grooves, have been turning up in mine shafts for decades. Their origin? Rock strata are a staggering 3 billion years old!

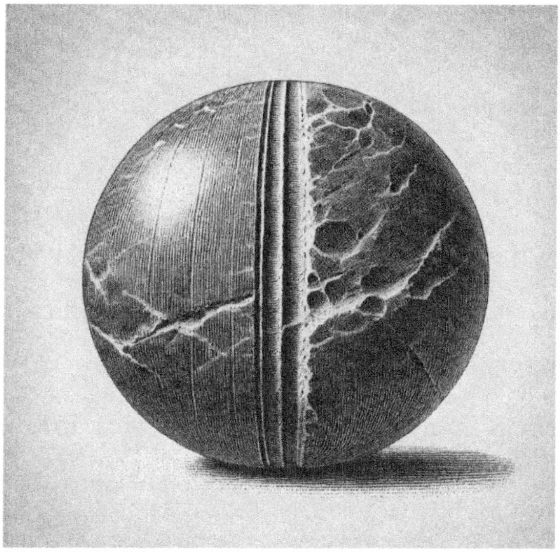

South African metallic spheres

Yet, the scientific community, seemingly content with its current understanding, has largely ignored these enigmatic artifacts.

Forbidden Archaeology: Unveiling the Cover-Up

These are not isolated incidents. Richard Thompson and Michael Cremo, in their monumental work "Forbidden Archaeology," have meticulously documented a mountain of similar cases. They paint a disturbing picture of a scientific establishment more concerned with preserving its theories than confronting inconvenient truths. Evidence that contradicts the accepted narrative is not just ignored; it's actively suppressed.

The prevailing theory of human evolution, with its neat timeline and gradual progression, is presented as an indisputable fact. But Cremo and Thompson argue that this is merely a carefully constructed consensus, a narrative that ignores a vast body of contradictory evidence.

The Case of George Carter

Take the story of George Carter, an archaeologist who unearthed hearths and crude stone tools in San Diego, California, dating back 80,000 to 90,000 years.

Despite support from experts, Carter faced scorn and ridicule. San Diego State University, the very institution in whose backyard this discovery was made, refused to even acknowledge the find. Harvard University went so far as to publicly denounce Carter in a course titled "Fantastic Archaeology."

A Pattern of Suppression

These cases reveal a pattern of arrogance and intellectual bullying within the academic elite. Scientists who dare to challenge the status quo are often ostracized and their careers ruined. The message is clear: toe the line or face the consequences.

Cremo and Thompson's "Forbidden Archaeology" has sent shockwaves through the scientific community. While some have dismissed it as "humbug," others have grudgingly acknowledged the weight of evidence it presents. As William Howells, writing in "Physical Anthropologist," admitted, the existence of modern humans millions of years ago would be "devastating" to the whole theory of evolution.

Beyond Evolution and Creationism

But "Forbidden Archaeology" doesn't simply challenge evolution; it calls for a complete re-evaluation of our understanding of human origins. Cremo, in his follow-up book "Human Devolution," proposes a more complex theory that incorporates elements of Darwinism, ancient astronaut theories, and even creationism, but goes beyond these simplistic frameworks.

Cremo and Thompson, both members of the Bhaktivedanta Institute, embarked on their research to find evidence to support the ancient Sanskrit writings of India, which describe human history stretching back millions of years. What they found, however, was far more expansive than they could have imagined. It was a hidden history, buried beneath layers of dogma and denial.

The Politics of Knowledge

Why this suppression of evidence? Cremo argues that it's about power and control. "There's a lot of social power connected with explaining who we are and what we are," he says. The scientific establishment has become a new priesthood, dictating the direction of our society and our understanding of the world.

But this worldview, with its mechanistic explanations and denial of the paranormal, is failing to account for the full spectrum of human experience. The environmental crisis, the political turmoil, the crisis in values – these are all symptoms of a worldview that has reached its limits.

A Cosmic Perspective

Cremo envisions a more expansive reality, one in which humans are part of a cosmic hierarchy of beings. This perspective, he argues, is supported by world mythologies and even the modern UFO phenomenon. The refusal of mainstream science to seriously engage with these phenomena is another indictment of its limitations.

Cataclysms and Planetary Amnesia

One of the key battlegrounds between orthodox and alternative views is the question of cataclysms. While mainstream science acknowledges catastrophic events in the distant past, it generally adheres to a gradualist view of human evolution. But researchers like Immanuel Velikovsky have argued that numerous cataclysms have punctuated human history, causing a kind of collective amnesia.

Cremo agrees, suggesting that ancient myths and oral traditions preserve memories of these catastrophes. But a "social amnesia," reinforced by those in power, prevents us from recognizing these as historical truths.

The Church of Progress

John Anthony West, another prominent figure in the alternative archaeology movement, sees modern civilization as a pale shadow of its predecessors. He criticizes the "Church of Progress" for its arrogance and its dismissal of ancient wisdom. West, along with geologist Robert Schoch, has been instrumental in challenging the age of the Sphinx, arguing that it shows evidence of water weathering and is therefore thousands of years older than conventionally believed.

Sphinx showing water weathering.

This challenge to the established timeline of Egyptian civilization has sparked a major controversy. But despite attempts to discredit their work, West and Schoch have gained increasing support, forcing the Egyptological establishment to engage with their ideas.

The Legacy of Schwaller de Lubicz

West draws inspiration from the work of R.A. Schwaller de Lubicz, a French philosopher and Egyptologist who spent years studying the Temple of Luxor. Schwaller de Lubicz argued that the ancient Egyptians possessed advanced knowledge of mathematics and harmony, including the Golden Section, long before the Greeks.

Temple of Luxor

West sees Schwaller de Lubicz's work as a "unified field theory" of ancient Egyptian wisdom, a key to understanding their sophisticated understanding of the universe.

Secrets of the Red Pyramid

West believes that the physical remains of a prehistoric civilization are not limited to the Sphinx. He points to several sites, including the Red Pyramid at Dahshur, as evidence of a much older, more advanced culture.

The Red Pyramid, attributed to the pharaoh Snefru, contains a peculiar chamber filled with water-weathered stones in a chaotic arrangement. West believes this chamber may be part of a much older structure, predating the pyramid itself.

Other Anomalies

West also points to other anomalies in Egyptian architecture, such as the two-stage construction of the Khafre pyramid and the weathered shaft near the Saqqara pyramid, as evidence of a lost civilization.

Khafre pyramid

He also highlights inconsistencies in the Cairo Museum's collection, such as a diorite vase from the Old Kingdom period that exhibits a level of precision impossible to achieve with the known tools of the time.

The Pyramid Texts

The pyramid texts, carved into the walls of Fifth and Sixth dynasty pyramids, are generally believed to be copies of much older sources. West, along with physicist and linguist Clesson H. Harvey, argues that these texts reveal an Egyptian religion tens of thousands of years old.

Towards a Proper Egyptology

West criticizes the current state of Egyptology, calling for a more meaningful approach to research. He suggests that scholars should focus on studying the harmonics and proportions of temples, the gestures in temple art, and the systematic effacements on temple walls.

Eoliths: Stones of Contention

The story of prehistoric technologies takes us back even further, to the enigmatic eoliths, or "dawn stones." These crude stone tools, found in Pliocene, Miocene, and even older strata, have been a source of controversy for over a century.

In the late 19th century, Benjamin Harrison, an amateur archaeologist, began unearthing these crude implements from the ancient river gravels of the Kent Plateau in England.

Kent Plateau eoliths

Working closely with renowned geologist Sir John Prestwich, Harrison meticulously documented his finds, which included not only eoliths but also more advanced Paleolithic and Neolithic tools.

The eoliths, with their seemingly simple modifications, sparked intense debate. Were these truly tools shaped by human hands, or merely naturally broken flints? Critics dismissed them as figments of Harrison's imagination, but prominent figures like Alfred Russel Wallace and Sir John Prestwich recognized the intentional flaking and retouching that distinguished them from ordinary rocks.

Despite the skepticism, Harrison persisted, conducting excavations funded by the British Association to demonstrate the in situ presence of eoliths within Pliocene gravels. His work gained further support from scientists like E.T. Newton and Ray E. Lankester, who recognized the clear signs of human intervention on these ancient stones.

J. Reid Moir and the East Anglia Enigma

The eolith controversy deepened with the discoveries of J. Reid Moir, a fellow of the Royal Anthropological Institute, along the southeast coast of England.

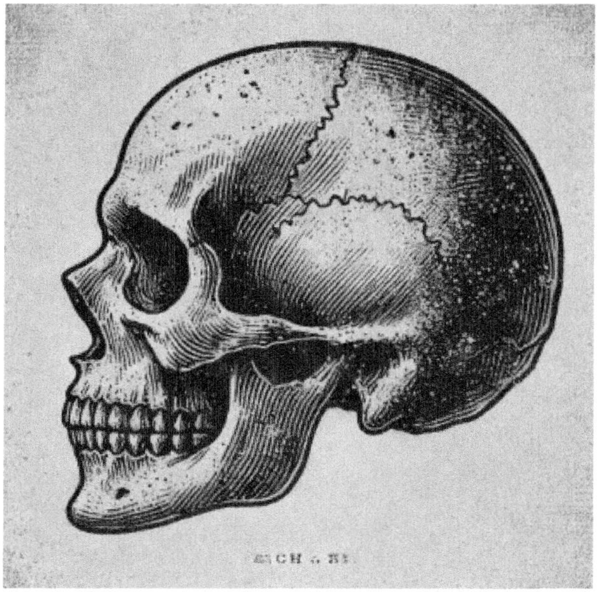

East Anglia eoliths

Moir unearthed flint implements from beneath the Red and Coralline Crags, geological formations dating back at least 2 million years.

Moir's finds, including the distinctive rostro-carinate tools, ignited further debate.

Rostrocarinate tool

While some dismissed them as natural formations, influential figures like Henri Breuil and Archibald Geikie recognized the clear signs of human craftsmanship.

The controversy reached a head with the discovery of stone tools in the Late Pliocene Red Crag formation at Foxhall. These tools, over 2 million years old, were found alongside a human jawbone, suggesting the presence of tool-making hominids in England far earlier than previously thought.

Despite the mounting evidence, resistance to Moir's findings persisted. Critics attributed the flaking to natural forces like geological pressure or iceberg activity. However, the International Institute of Anthropology formed a commission of experts who, after examining the sites and the artifacts, concluded that the flaking was undoubtedly of human origin.

The Calico Controversy

The eolith question resurfaced in the Americas with the controversial Calico site in California's Mojave Desert.

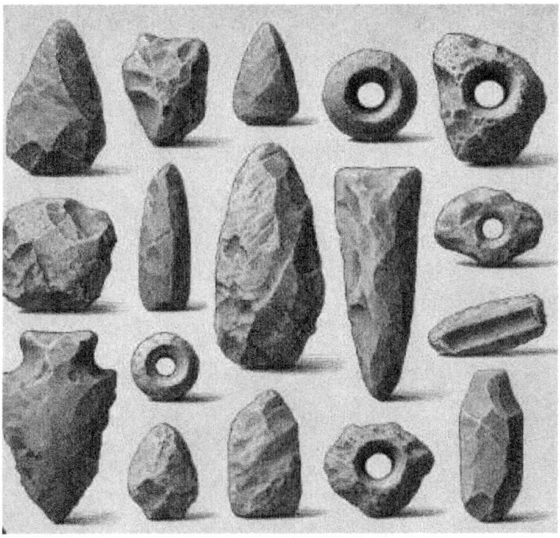

Calico site eoliths

Excavations led by Ruth D. Simpson unearthed thousands of eolith-like artifacts from layers dated as old as 200,000 years.

Despite support from prominent figures like Louis Leakey and Phillip Tobias, the Calico finds were largely dismissed by mainstream archaeologists as geofacts – products of natural processes rather than human intervention.

Toca da Esperanca and Monte Verde: Shifting the Paradigm

However, discoveries in Brazil and Chile lent credence to the Calico finds and challenged the conventional timeline of human presence in the Americas.

In Brazil, the Toca da Esperanca cave yielded crude stone tools associated with Pleistocene mammals, dating back over 200,000 years.

This discovery, reported by renowned archaeologist Henry de Lumley, suggested that humans had arrived in the Americas far earlier than previously thought.

The Monte Verde site in Chile, although younger, provided further evidence of early human presence in South America. This site, dated between 12,500 and 13,500 years old, contained not only stone tools but also preserved organic materials, including wooden tools, architectural foundations, and hearths.

Monte Verde site artifacts

The Monte Verde findings demonstrated that even the crudest stone tools could be associated with advanced cultures.

Eoliths in Asia and the Question of Human Ancestry

Eolith-like implements have also been found in Asia, challenging the prevailing "Out of Africa" theory of human origins. In

Pakistan, crude chopping tools dating back 2 million years were unearthed, suggesting the presence of hominids outside Africa far earlier than conventionally accepted.

Pakistan eoliths

Similar discoveries in Siberia and India, with tools dating back 1.5 to 2.5 million years, further challenge the established timeline of human migration.

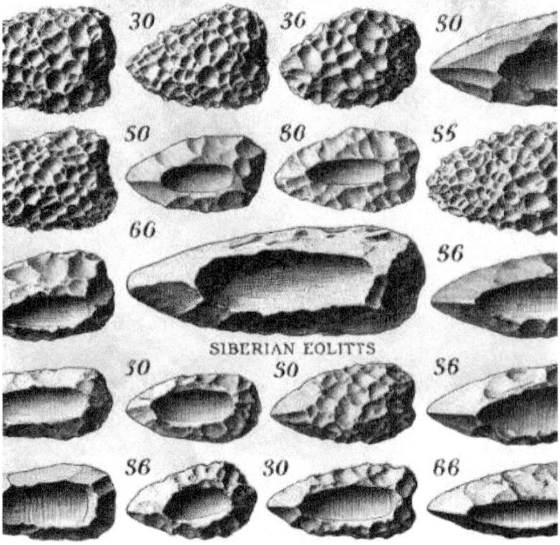

Siberian eoliths

Even more intriguing is the discovery of a crude hand-axe in the Miocene Nagri formation in India, dating back over 5 million years.

This finding raises fundamental questions about the very origins of tool-making hominids.

Who Made the Eoliths?

The persistent discoveries of eoliths and other crude stone tools across vast periods and geography raise a crucial question: who made them?

The conventional answer is that these tools were crafted by early hominids like Homo habilis. However, the crudest tools from Olduvai Gorge, attributed to Homo habilis, are virtually indistinguishable from eoliths found in Europe and elsewhere.

Furthermore, the discovery of anatomically modern human fossils in strata as old as the lower levels of Olduvai Gorge suggests that Homo sapiens may have been present far earlier than conventionally thought.

This raises the possibility that Homo sapiens, not just earlier hominids, were responsible for some, if not all, of the eoliths and crude stone tools found around the world. This challenges the linear progression of human evolution and suggests a far more complex and ancient history than currently accepted.

The Implications of Prehistoric Technologies

The evidence presented in this chapter paints a picture of a prehistoric world teeming with technological innovation, stretching back millions of years. The implications of these findings are profound:

- **Human origins may be far more ancient and complex than currently believed.** The presence of sophisticated tools and even anatomically modern human fossils in extremely old geological strata challenges the established timeline of human evolution.
- **Advanced civilizations may have existed in the distant past, leaving behind only subtle traces.** The enigmatic eoliths, along with other anomalous finds, hint at the possibility of lost civilizations whose technologies and cultures remain largely unknown.
- **The suppression of evidence has hindered our understanding of the true history of humanity.** The resistance to accepting evidence that contradicts the prevailing narrative has created a distorted and incomplete picture of our past.

The study of prehistoric technologies is not merely an academic exercise; it is a quest to uncover the hidden history of humanity and to understand our true origins and our place in the universe. The evidence presented in this chapter challenges us to rethink our assumptions and embrace a more expansive view of our past.

Chapter 5: The Mystery of Ancient Egypt

The ancient Egyptian civilization stands as one of the most enigmatic and compelling cultures in human history. Known for its monumental architecture, sophisticated society, and profound contributions to mathematics, astronomy, and the arts, Egypt has long captivated historians, archaeologists, and laypeople alike. Yet, beneath the surface of what is commonly accepted lies contradictions and unanswered questions that challenge the very foundations of our understanding. Recent discoveries have unveiled a plethora of artifacts and insights suggesting that ancient Egypt possessed a level of technology and knowledge that defies conventional historical narratives. This chapter delves into these revelations, exploring the implications of a society that may have harnessed advanced techniques to create wonders that continue to baffle modern scholars.

The Conventional Narrative: Tombs or Power Plants?

Giza pyramids and Sphinx

For centuries, Egyptologists have championed the idea that the Great Pyramid of Giza and its counterparts served primarily as tombs for pharaohs. This narrative has been entrenched in academic circles, perpetuated by the lack of substantial evidence supporting alternative theories. However, as new data emerges, it becomes increasingly evident that the pyramids may have had purposes far beyond mere burial sites. Christopher Dunn's groundbreaking work, *The Giza Power Plant*, posits that the pyramids functioned as sophisticated energy machines, capable of harnessing acoustic and vibrational energies from the Earth.

Dunn's theory suggests that the Great Pyramid was meticulously designed to resonate with the Earth's natural frequencies. It is believed that the intricate chambers and passageways within the pyramid were not simply architectural feats but were integral to a complex system that converted vibrational energy into usable power. The King's Chamber, with its precise dimensions and granite composition, is posited as the heart of this energy plant. The evidence supporting this theory lies not only in the construction itself but also in the unique geological and acoustic properties of the pyramid's materials.

The Great Pyramid: A Monument to Lost Technology

The Great Pyramid of Giza, a towering testament to human ingenuity, has long been a source of wonder and speculation.

Great Pyramid

Its massive scale, precise alignment, and intricate internal structure have defied explanation for centuries.

Conventional theories attribute its construction to primitive tools and techniques, and a vast workforce laboring for decades with copper chisels and stone hammers. But these explanations fall woefully short when confronted with the sheer precision and sophistication of the pyramid's construction.

The Great Pyramid's base, covering an area of 13 acres, is leveled to within less than an inch. Its sides are aligned to the cardinal points with astonishing accuracy. Its inner chambers contain granite blocks weighing up to 70 tons, fitted together with such precision that a razor blade cannot be inserted between them.

How could a supposedly Bronze Age civilization achieve such feats of engineering? The answer, it seems, lies in a lost technology, one that challenges our assumptions about the capabilities of our ancient ancestors.

Advanced Machining in Ancient Egypt

Close examination of the granite artifacts found throughout Egypt reveals further evidence of advanced machining techniques.

Granite sarcophagus in the Great Pyramid

The smooth, flat surfaces, the precise cuts, and the intricate details point to the use of tools and techniques far beyond the capabilities of copper chisels and stone hammers.

Sir William Flinders Petrie, the pioneering Egyptologist, recognized this discrepancy over a century ago. In his book "Pyramids and Temples of Giza," he expressed astonishment at the precision of the ancient Egyptians' stonework, suggesting they possessed methods "we are only now coming to understand."

Yet, modern Egyptologists continue to cling to the notion that primitive tools and techniques were sufficient to produce these marvels of engineering. They propose that the ancients used dolerite balls to "bash" the granite into shape, a ludicrous explanation when confronted with the intricate hieroglyphs and precise contours found on many artifacts.

Hieroglyphs are carved in granite.

The evidence points to the use of advanced machining techniques, including lathes, milling machines, ultrasonic drills, and high-speed saws.

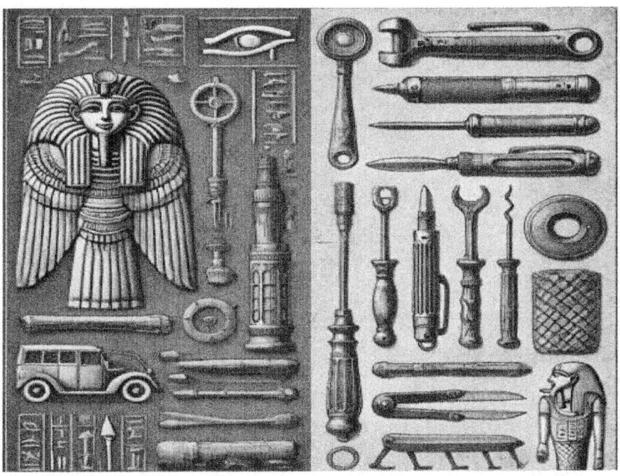

Ancient Egyptian tools, juxtaposed with modern equivalents

These tools, however, are absent from the archaeological record, conveniently ignored by those determined to maintain the conventional narrative.

The Giza Power Plant: A Controversial Theory

If the ancient Egyptians possessed such advanced machining capabilities, what was their power source? This question has led to a controversial theory: that the Great Pyramid itself was a massive power plant, harnessing the Earth's natural energies to generate electricity.

Christopher Dunn, a manufacturing engineer, has spent decades researching this theory, meticulously analyzing the pyramid's design and the artifacts found within it. In his book "The Giza Power Plant," he presents a compelling case for the pyramid's true purpose.

Dunn argues that the pyramid was designed to resonate with the Earth's natural frequencies, capturing vibrational energy and converting it into microwave energy. This energy, he suggests, was then used to power the advanced machines used to create the granite artifacts found throughout Egypt.

Dunn's theory has been met with skepticism and ridicule from the Egyptological establishment. But his meticulous analysis and the growing body of evidence he has amassed cannot be easily dismissed.

The Challenges of Conventional Methods

Traditional Egyptology has often relied on outdated assumptions regarding the methods employed by the ancient builders. Egyptologists typically cite the use of simple tools, such as copper chisels and stone hammers, to explain the remarkable precision of the pyramid's construction. Yet, experimental archaeology has consistently failed to replicate the same level of craftsmanship using these primitive tools. Dunn emphasizes this failure as indicative of a deeper issue: the potential existence of advanced machining techniques that have been largely ignored or dismissed.

Sir William Flinders Petrie, the father of modern Egyptology, recognized early on that the tools displayed in museums were insufficient to account for the precision and complexity of the artifacts found in Egypt. He noted that the ancient craftsmen must have utilized techniques and tools that, although no longer present in the archaeological record, were far more advanced than contemporary scholars are willing to acknowledge. This raises critical questions: What knowledge was lost? How advanced was ancient Egyptian technology?

The Queen's Chamber: A Chemical Factory?

Dunn's theory begins with the Queen's Chamber, located deep within the Great Pyramid.

Queen's chamber

This chamber, with its peculiar shafts and mysterious "door," has long puzzled researchers.

Dunn proposes that the Queen's Chamber was a chemical factory, producing hydrogen gas through a carefully controlled reaction. This hydrogen, he suggests, was then channeled to the King's Chamber, the heart of the power plant.

The King's Chamber: A Resonant Cavity

The King's Chamber, constructed entirely of granite, is another key component of Dunn's theory.

King's Chamber

He argues that this chamber was designed as a resonant cavity, amplifying the vibrational energy captured by the pyramid.

The granite itself, with its high quartz content, acts as a piezoelectric material, converting mechanical stress into electrical energy. As the chamber vibrates, it generates an electromagnetic field, further energizing the hydrogen atoms within.

The Grand Gallery: An Acoustic Amplifier

The Grand Gallery, a soaring passageway leading to the King's Chamber, plays a crucial role in Dunn's theory.

He argues that this gallery was designed as an acoustic amplifier, focusing sound waves toward the King's Chamber.

The gallery's corbeled walls and ratchet-style ceiling create a series of Helmholtz resonators, amplifying specific frequencies and channeling them toward the King's Chamber.

The Power Plant in Action

According to Dunn's theory, the Great Pyramid operated as follows:

1. Chemicals were pumped into the Queen's Chamber, generating hydrogen gas.
2. The pyramid was vibrated at its resonant frequency, capturing the Earth's natural energies.
3. The Grand Gallery amplified these vibrations, focusing them towards the King's Chamber.
4. The King's Chamber, acting as a resonant cavity, further amplified the vibrations and generated an electromagnetic field.
5. The energized hydrogen atoms within the King's Chamber emitted microwave energy.
6. This microwave energy was channeled through the pyramid's shafts to the outside, where it was used to power the ancient Egyptians' advanced technology.

Evidence for the Power Plant Theory

Dunn's theory is supported by a growing body of evidence, including:

- The precise dimensions and alignment of the Great Pyramid, suggest it was designed to resonate with the Earth's natural frequencies.
- The peculiar features of the Queen's Chamber, indicate it was used for a chemical process.

- The resonant properties of the King's Chamber, suggest it was used to generate an electromagnetic field.
- The acoustic design of the Grand Gallery, suggests it was used to amplify sound waves.
- The presence of scorch marks and heat damage within the pyramid, suggest a powerful energy source was once active within.

The Implications of the Giza Power Plant

If Dunn's theory is correct, it would revolutionize our understanding of ancient Egypt and the capabilities of prehistoric civilizations. It would suggest that the ancient Egyptians possessed a level of technological sophistication far beyond what we have imagined.

Furthermore, it would raise profound questions about the origins of this technology and the fate of the civilization that created it. Was this technology developed independently, or was it inherited from an even older, more advanced civilization? And what caused the demise of this civilization, leaving behind only enigmatic monuments and tantalizing clues?

It is critical to recognize that the narrative of decline does not negate the accomplishments of the ancient Egyptians. Rather, it emphasizes the potential for civilizations to rise and fall based on their mastery of knowledge and technology. This serves as a cautionary tale for contemporary society: the technologies we take for granted today may not endure forever. Just as the ancient Egyptians built their marvels, so too must we consider how our technological advancements might be preserved or lost to time.

Advanced Machining and Evidence of Lost Technology

One of the most striking pieces of evidence supporting the existence of advanced technology in ancient Egypt is the precision of granite artifacts. Dunn's research, along with that of other experts, has demonstrated that the tools required to create these artifacts would have been far more sophisticated than copper chisels and stone balls. The existence of finely detailed hieroglyphs, smooth surfaces, and intricate carvings suggests that the builders employed techniques akin to modern machining.

In one notable instance, Dunn examined a sarcophagus inside the pyramid of Khafre, discovering internal surfaces that were remarkably smooth and flat, a level of precision that challenges our understanding of ancient craftsmanship. The findings indicate that the ancient Egyptians may have utilized sophisticated tools capable of achieving the tolerances that modern manufacturers strive for. Furthermore, the presence of tool marks resembling those produced by lathe turning raises the possibility that these craftsmen had access to machinery capable of executing precise operations on hard materials like granite.

The Debate Continues

The debate over the true purpose of the Great Pyramid and the level of technology possessed by the ancient Egyptians continues to rage. However, the evidence for advanced machining and the possibility of a lost power source cannot be easily dismissed.

The sands of Egypt still hold many secrets, whispers of a lost technological heritage that challenges our assumptions about the past. As we continue to explore these ancient wonders, we may yet uncover the truth about the Giza power plant and the true capabilities of the ancient Egyptians.

Chapter 6: The Enigma of Sumerian Civilization

Sumer. The very word evokes a sense of deep time, of a civilization shrouded in the mists of prehistory. Emerging seemingly out of nowhere in the Mesopotamian plains around 3500 B.C.E., the Sumerians bequeathed to the world a staggering array of innovations: writing, the wheel, complex mathematics, astronomy, advanced agriculture, and the very concept of the city itself.

Royal Standard of Ur

But how did this sudden blossoming of civilization occur? How did a people, supposedly just emerging from the Stone Age, achieve such a profound leap in knowledge and technology? The conventional narrative, with its emphasis on gradual development and linear progress, simply cannot account for the Sumerian enigma.

Missing Links in the Chain of Progress

We are told that agriculture was the catalyst for the Sumerian revolution. But this explanation raises more questions than it answers. How did people with no prior experience with cultivating grains suddenly master the complexities of farming, irrigation, and crop hybridization?

ancient Sumerian agricultural scene

The Sumerians were not just farmers; they were also skilled engineers, architects, and astronomers. They built massive ziggurats, developed intricate irrigation systems, and possessed a detailed knowledge of the cosmos.

Where are the precursors to these advancements? Where are the smaller ziggurats, the simpler irrigation canals, and the rudimentary astronomical observations that would demonstrate a gradual evolution of knowledge and skill?

The Sumerian civilization appears fully formed, a sudden burst of innovation with no clear antecedents. This abrupt emergence challenges our understanding of human progress and suggests the possibility of external influences or forgotten chapters in our history.

Sitchin's Controversial Claim

Zecharia Sitchin, a scholar of ancient languages and author of "The Earth Chronicles" series, offers a controversial but compelling explanation for the Sumerian enigma. He argues that the Sumerians interacted with extraterrestrial visitors, the Anunnaki, who played a crucial role in their rapid advancement.

Sitchin bases his theory on a literal interpretation of ancient Sumerian texts, which describe the Anunnaki as "gods" who descended from the heavens and imparted knowledge and technology to the Sumerians.

Anunnaki depiction from an ancient Sumerian tablet

While Sitchin's theory is often dismissed as fringe, it provides a possible answer to the perplexing question of Sumerian origins. If the Sumerians were indeed guided by extraterrestrial beings, it could explain their sudden leap in knowledge and technological prowess.

The Puzzle of Pre-Sumerian Culture

Even if we accept the possibility of extraterrestrial influence, the mystery of Sumer deepens when we consider the evidence for even older civilizations in the region. Archaeological excavations have revealed traces of cultures predating the Sumerians, possessing advanced knowledge and technologies.

For example, the discovery of Göbekli Tepe in Turkey, a complex of massive stone circles dating back to 10,000 B.C.E., challenges the notion that the Sumerians were the first civilization in the region.

These pre-Sumerian cultures raise the possibility of a long-forgotten chapter in human history, a time when advanced civilizations flourished and then vanished, leaving behind only tantalizing clues.

The Anunnaki and Human Origins

Sitchin's theory extends beyond Sumer, encompassing the origins of humanity itself. He argues that the Anunnaki genetically engineered humans to serve as their workforce, a claim supported by ancient Sumerian texts that describe the creation of humans from clay.

This genetic manipulation, Sitchin argues, could explain the sudden appearance of Homo sapiens in the fossil record, a phenomenon that has puzzled paleoanthropologists for decades.

The Flood and the Loss of Knowledge

Sitchin also identifies a cataclysmic flood in ancient Sumerian texts, an event that mirrors the biblical story of Noah's Ark. He argues that this flood, which he dates to around 11,000 B.C.E., wiped out advanced civilizations that existed before the Sumerians.

This catastrophic event, Sitchin suggests, could explain the loss of knowledge and the apparent "resetting" of human civilization, forcing humanity to rebuild from scratch.

Unearthing the Forgotten Past

Until the late nineteenth century, Sumer was largely considered a myth, a footnote in the annals of history. However, archaeological discoveries in places like Nineveh and Ur forced historians to reconsider their preconceived notions. Artifacts unearthed from these sites have reshaped our understanding of ancient Mesopotamia and demonstrated that Sumerians were not only real but were at the forefront of human development.

The Sumerians introduced writing, established urban centers and created complex social structures. Their contributions, including the wheel, irrigation systems, and the earliest forms of literature, underscore their role as pioneers of civilization. Yet, despite these accomplishments, we find ourselves questioning how such advancements occurred in such a compressed time frame.

Sumerian writing tablets

The Leap from Hunter-Gatherers to Civilization

The transition from nomadic hunter-gatherer societies to settled agricultural communities was not merely a shift in lifestyle; it represented a seismic change in human existence. Archaeological evidence suggests that this transformation occurred suddenly, raising significant questions about its causes. How did Stone Age peoples, who relied on hunting and gathering, suddenly acquire the knowledge and skills necessary to cultivate crops and domesticate animals?

The prevailing narrative suggests that agricultural practices developed over millennia, yet the evidence tells a different story. The Sumerians cultivated grains and created complex agricultural systems that seemingly appeared out of nowhere. This abrupt shift is akin to a technological revolution occurring overnight. What could have prompted such a radical departure from established norms?

Image illustrating the contrast between Stone Age life and early agricultural practices.

The Enigma of Grains and Domestication

It is essential to address the issue of grains, the cornerstone of agriculture. Our Stone Age ancestors did not consume grains, relying instead on wild meats and plants. When we examine the diets of early humans, we find that grains were largely absent. So, how did they transition to a grain-based diet, and how did they come to understand the processes of planting, harvesting, and processing these crops?

The timeline for the domestication of grains and the advent of agriculture suggests a level of knowledge and sophistication that hunter-gatherers would not have possessed. We must ask ourselves: where did this expertise originate? The knowledge required to hybridize and cultivate grains points to a sudden leap in human understanding, contradicting the gradual evolution we typically associate with human progress.

The Role of Knowledge Transfer

One compelling theory to consider is the possibility of knowledge transfer from the advanced civilizations that preceded Sumer. Could there have been an earlier civilization with agricultural knowledge that was lost to time? The absence of intermediary steps in the archaeological record raises significant questions about how Sumerian society could develop so rapidly.

As we analyze the Sumerian advancements, we must also scrutinize the archaeological record for signs of precursors to this civilization. Where are the smaller-scale agricultural communities that would logically precede Sumer? The lack of evidence suggests that either Sumer was an anomaly or that we are missing a crucial piece of the puzzle.

A Civilization Built on Myths?

In exploring the enigma of Sumer, we encounter ancient texts that offer insights into the Sumerian worldview. Myths and legends, such as the Epic of Gilgamesh, not only provide glimpses into their culture but also hint at the deep-rooted beliefs that shaped their civilization. These texts often contain kernels of truth obscured by layers of myth and legend.

The existence of flood myths across multiple cultures points to a shared experience or collective memory of catastrophic events. The Sumerians' accounts of a great flood, echoed in other civilizations, provoke questions about historical accuracy and the transmission of stories across generations. Were these narratives merely tales spun to explain the unexplainable, or do they contain elements of historical fact?

The Epic of Gilgamesh

The Limits of Conventional Explanations

Traditional historical narratives struggle to account for the rapid advancements made by the Sumerians. As we delve deeper into the enigma of Sumer, we must confront the limitations of orthodox theories that often rely on accepted paradigms. The sudden emergence of Sumerian civilization challenges the established timelines and raises the specter of alternative explanations.

Many historians and archaeologists adhere to the belief that civilizations evolve gradually, yet Sumer contradicts this principle. The sudden creation of complex societal structures, advanced technologies, and monumental architecture cannot simply be attributed to natural progression. We must explore the possibility that hidden forces, whether human or otherwise, played a role in shaping this enigmatic civilization.

The Role of External Influences

The suggestion that Sumerian civilization could have been influenced by external forces raises a host of controversial questions. Could advanced knowledge have been imparted to the Sumerians by travelers, traders, or even extraterrestrial beings? While such theories may seem far-fetched to some, the inexplicable gaps in our understanding of early civilization compel us to consider all possibilities.

Zecharia Sitchin's works, for instance, propose that ancient astronauts visited Earth and influenced early human civilizations. While his theories remain contentious, they challenge us to reevaluate our assumptions about the origins of human knowledge and technology. We must be open to the idea that Sumer may not represent a linear progression but rather a complex interplay of ideas, influences, and possibly even extraterrestrial contact.

The Sumerian Legacy

Despite the mysteries surrounding their origins, the Sumerians left an indelible mark on human history. Their innovations in writing, mathematics, astronomy, and agriculture laid the foundation for subsequent civilizations, including the Egyptians, Babylonians, and Assyrians.

The Sumerian legacy is a testament to the ingenuity and resilience of the human spirit. But it also serves as a reminder of the fragility of civilization and the possibility of lost chapters in our history.

Unanswered Questions

The enigma of Sumerian civilization continues to challenge our understanding of the past. Many questions remain unanswered:

- How did the Sumerians achieve such a rapid advancement in knowledge and technology?
- Was their civilization influenced by extraterrestrial visitors, as Sitchin suggests?
- What happened to the pre-Sumerian cultures that existed in the region?
- How did the Sumerian civilization ultimately collapse?

Sumerian civilization, despite its mysterious origins, left an indelible mark on human history. Their innovations in agriculture, writing, and technology laid the foundation for the civilizations that followed.

But perhaps their greatest legacy is the challenge they pose to our understanding of the past. The enigma of Sumer compels us to question our assumptions, seek out forbidden knowledge, and explore the hidden depths of human history.

Chapter 7: The Hidden History of the Americas

The history of the Americas, particularly Central America, is filled with enigmas that mainstream science often fails to address. Here we are unveiling the hidden narratives of ancient civilizations, especially the Olmecs and the Maya, exploring their origins and connections that challenge established historical frameworks. By dissecting these cultures, we delve into a narrative that compels us to reconsider the trajectory of human civilization and the potential for ancient global interactions.

The Enigma of the Olmec Civilization

The Olmec civilization, often referred to as the "mother culture" of Mesoamerica, emerged around 1200 BCE in what is now southern Mexico. Their legacy is not only marked by monumental architecture but also by a series of artifacts that defy easy categorization. The colossal basalt heads, weighing between five and twenty-five tons, and the intricately carved stelae depicting figures with distinctly non-Mesoamerican features raise pressing questions about their creators.

Mainstream archaeology struggles to offer coherent explanations for these artifacts, often relegating them to mere curiosities without fully grappling with their implications. Who were these people? What cultural exchanges might have occurred? The absence of written records from the Olmec period adds another layer of complexity to these inquiries. Scholars often resort to theories that diminish the Olmecs' significance, but as Will Hart noted, the failure to engage with the evidence presents a fundamental contradiction in scientific inquiry.

In Genesis 11, we encounter a historical perspective that might provide context for these puzzling artifacts. The passage describes a time when humanity shared a common language and purpose, suggesting that the Olmecs could have been part of a broader, interconnected world. However, mainstream archaeology tends to ignore such implications, adhering to a narrative that simplifies the complexities of cultural development.

The Origins of the Olmecs: A Closer Look

The origins of the Olmec civilization are obscured by a veil of mystery, prompting inquiries into their true beginnings. While mainstream theories often posit a local emergence of Olmec culture, there is mounting evidence suggesting they may have descended from an earlier, more widespread civilization. This idea is not just speculation; it aligns with patterns observed in ancient human migrations.

Recent genetic studies reveal that the indigenous peoples of the Americas share common ancestry with populations from Asia, indicating a migration that occurred thousands of years ago via the Bering Land Bridge. This connection establishes a lineage that links the Olmecs and their descendants to broader patterns of human migration. It raises profound questions about how these early populations might have interacted with other global civilizations, laying the groundwork for the sophisticated societies that would later flourish.

Colossal Olmec head

The striking features found in Olmec art, particularly the Negroid characteristics of the colossal heads, have prompted speculation about the possible influence of African civilizations. Some scholars argue that there may have been trans-oceanic contact, suggesting that the Olmecs might have been part of a larger network of trade and cultural exchange that spanned the globe. This theory challenges the notion of isolated ancient cultures, proposing instead that the Olmecs were one piece of a much larger puzzle.

The Maya: Masters of Time and Astronomy

The Maya civilization, which rose to prominence around 250 CE, offers a remarkable narrative of achievement that defies simplistic characterizations of "primitive" societies. The Maya constructed monumental cities, developed complex political structures, and possessed an extraordinary understanding of astronomy and mathematics. Their calendar systems—particularly the Tzolk'in (sacred calendar), Haab' (civil calendar), and the Long Count—demonstrate a sophisticated grasp of celestial cycles that surpasses many contemporary cultures.

What is often overlooked is the depth of their timekeeping methods. The Maya meticulously tracked celestial events, achieving remarkable precision in their calendrical systems. Their understanding of the synodic period of Venus, calculated at 584 Earth days, showcases their advanced astronomical knowledge. The question arises: how could a civilization that lacked modern scientific tools attain such insights?

Some researchers propose that this knowledge was inherited from earlier civilizations, perhaps even those with advanced technologies. This notion challenges the prevailing paradigm that dismisses the possibility of significant cultural exchanges across continents in ancient times. Instead, it suggests a continuity of knowledge passed down through generations, possibly linking the Maya with earlier, forgotten civilizations.

Ancient Mayan pyramid at Tikal

The Infrastructure of Civilization: Sacbe and Beyond

Further investigations into Mayan civilization reveal their expertise in engineering and infrastructure. The sacbe, or white roads, crisscrossed the dense jungles of the Yucatán Peninsula, forming a network that connected ceremonial centers, agricultural lands, and communities. These roads, meticulously constructed and paved with limestone, indicate an advanced understanding of civil engineering.

James O'Kon's groundbreaking work on the longest-known suspension bridge in the ancient world highlights the sophistication of Mayan engineering. His findings demonstrate that the Maya were not merely surviving in their environment; they were actively shaping it. The engineering techniques employed for the bridge reflect a level of technical knowledge that defies the characterization of a "Stone Age" society.

The Consequences of a Paradigm Shift

The implications of this hidden history extend far beyond academic discourse. Recognizing the sophistication of ancient civilizations in the Americas necessitates a paradigm shift in how we understand human history. It challenges our assumptions about cultural evolution, technological progress, and the interconnectedness of societies throughout history.

The prevailing scientific narrative, often steeped in Eurocentrism, has marginalized the achievements of non-Western cultures. This oversight distorts our understanding of the past and perpetuates a cycle of ignorance about the complexities of human civilization. As we peel back the layers of history, we must confront uncomfortable truths about the origins and developments of these advanced cultures.

Lost Civilizations and Catastrophic Events

Throughout history, many civilizations have been shaped by catastrophic events. The myths and oral traditions of various cultures, including the Maya, recount tales of great floods and disasters that could provide insights into historical events that led to the transformation or collapse of advanced societies.

References to cataclysmic floods exist in approximately 230 different cultures worldwide. This widespread motif suggests that such events were not isolated incidents but rather shared experiences of human civilizations. The Mayans, for instance, spoke of a land to the east that was destroyed—a memory echoing throughout their history.

The True and Hidden History of the Americas

As we explore the hidden history of the Americas, we must grapple with the true origins of its ancient cultures. The Americas were not merely a blank slate for European colonizers; they were home to vibrant societies with rich histories and traditions. The initial inhabitants of the Americas migrated from Asia, utilizing the Bering Land Bridge during the last Ice Age. Over thousands of years, these early populations spread across the continent, adapting to diverse environments and developing complex societies. The genetic legacy of these early migrations continues to be reflected in the modern-day populations of North and South America.

However, the story does not end there. As these cultures flourished, there were likely interactions with other civilizations, both across the Pacific and the Atlantic. Recent studies have suggested the possibility of trans-oceanic contact, which could mean that the indigenous cultures of the Americas were influenced by ancient maritime trade routes that connected them to Africa, Asia, and even Europe.

This interconnectedness raises questions about the development of cultural practices, technological advancements, and social structures among the indigenous peoples. For instance, the sophistication of agricultural techniques seen in the Maya and their knowledge of astronomy could hint at exchanges with other ancient civilizations that possessed similar knowledge.

Reconstructing Our Understanding of Indigenous Civilizations

To reconstruct the history of the Americas accurately, we must look beyond the artifacts and explore the cultural narratives passed down through generations. Oral traditions hold immense value, providing insights into the lives, beliefs, and struggles of ancient civilizations. These narratives often contain truths about migrations, conflicts, and interactions that mainstream history overlooks.

The legends of the Maya, for instance, reveal their deep connection to the cosmos and their reverence for nature. These stories illustrate not only their understanding of astronomy but also their profound relationship with the environment. The Maya believed that their civilization was intricately linked to the cycles of nature, and their agricultural practices were aligned with celestial events.

The indigenous peoples of the Americas were not static; they were dynamic societies that evolved and adapted, leaving behind rich legacies that continue to resonate today.

The Search for Truth: A Call to Action

The unearthing of these historical mysteries compels us to challenge the status quo in historical narratives. Instead of dismissing anomalies and sidelining artifacts that do not fit established theories, scholars and researchers must adopt an open-minded approach to history.

We must ask ourselves: What if the data we have is a piece of a larger puzzle, a fragment of a narrative that has yet to be fully understood? What if the civilizations of the Americas were part of a grander story of human development, interconnectedness, and knowledge sharing that transcends geographical boundaries?

Engaging with these questions is not just an academic exercise; it is an urgent need in our quest for truth. The fabric of human history is woven with the threads of diverse cultures and civilizations that have risen and fallen. By examining the evidence before us, we can begin to weave a more comprehensive narrative that honors the complexity of our shared past.

Part II: The Suppression of Knowledge

We've journeyed through the ruins of lost civilizations, unearthed artifacts that defy conventional timelines, and glimpsed the possibility of advanced prehistoric technologies. But there's a darker side to this pursuit of forbidden history – a deliberate and systematic effort to suppress knowledge, to keep inconvenient truths hidden from public view.

This suppression is not a new phenomenon. Throughout history, powerful forces have sought to control the flow of information, to shape the narrative of the past to suit their agendas. Secret societies, religious institutions, governments, and even the scientific establishment itself have all played a role in this grand conspiracy of silence.

In this section, we'll explore the shadowy world of knowledge suppression, exposing the mechanisms and motivations behind this age-old practice. We'll explore the role of secret societies, the Vatican's hidden archives, the lost libraries of the ancient world, the suppression of scientific discoveries, and the untold story of the World Wars.

Prepare to be shocked, angered, and perhaps even frightened as we lift the veil on a hidden history that has been deliberately kept from us. The truth, as they say, is often stranger than fiction.

Chapter 8: The Role of Secret Societies

Throughout history, secret societies have operated in the shadows, influencing events and shaping cultures while often remaining hidden from the public eye. These groups have included some of the most powerful figures in history, from kings and queens to founding fathers and modern-day leaders. Understanding their role requires diving deep into the enigmatic histories, rituals, and networks that define these organizations. In this chapter, we will explore five notable secret societies: the Knights Templar, Freemasons, Illuminati, Skull and Bones, and Bilderberg, uncovering the impact they've had on world history and the continuing relevance of their legacies today.

1. The Knights Templar

Seal of the Knights Templar

Origins and Rise to Power

The Knights Templar was established in the early 12th century, around 1118, by Hugues de Payens, a French knight. Formed ostensibly to protect Christian pilgrims traveling to the Holy Land during the Crusades, the Templars quickly evolved into a powerful military and financial organization. Headquartered at the Temple Mount in Jerusalem, the order adopted a strict code of conduct emphasizing chastity, poverty, and obedience. Members were expected to live disciplined lives, abstaining from gambling, alcohol, and even swearing.

Their military prowess was impressive, and they became known for their distinctive white mantles emblazoned with a red cross. But what set the Templars apart was their ability to amass wealth and influence. They developed a sophisticated banking system that allowed pilgrims to deposit money in their home countries and withdraw it upon arrival in the Holy Land. This financial acumen positioned them as a major economic force in medieval Europe.

In 1139, Pope Innocent II issued a Papal Bull exempting the Knights Templar from paying taxes, granting them unique privileges. This elevation in status allowed them to operate independently, answering only to the Pope. At their peak, the Knights Templar owned vast tracts of land, a fleet of ships, and substantial financial resources, even lending money to kings.

The Downfall of the Knights Templar

Knight Templar

Despite their power, the Knights Templar faced growing resentment from monarchs who sought to curb their influence. After the fall of Acre in 1291, the order withdrew to Paris, focusing on their banking operations. However, in a shocking turn of events, King Philip IV of France, deeply indebted to the Templars, orchestrated a campaign to dismantle the order. On

Friday, October 13, 1307, hundreds of Templar knights were arrested, tortured, and coerced into confessing to heresy and other crimes, including bizarre accusations like sodomy and devil worship.

Under pressure from Philip, Pope Clement V formally dissolved the Knights Templar in 1312, redistributing their wealth and assets. Many Templars were executed, and the order's secrets were buried with them. This dramatic downfall has given rise to numerous conspiracy theories, particularly regarding their alleged guardianship of sacred relics like the Holy Grail and the Shroud of Turin. Modern interpretations of Templar history have fueled popular culture, inspiring novels and films that continue to captivate the public imagination.

The Legacy of the Knights Templar

Today, the legacy of the Knights Templar endures in various forms, from Masonic symbols to historical reinterpretations. Their story serves as a reminder of the intersection between power, faith, and wealth, and raises critical questions about the nature of secrecy and authority in society. As we explore other secret societies, we will see how the Templars' influence set a precedent for the power dynamics that would evolve over the centuries.

2. The Freemasons

A depiction of a masonic ritual taking place

Historical Context and Development

The Freemasons have long been intertwined with the fabric of American history, with several Founding Fathers, including George Washington and Benjamin Franklin, as members. Their roots can be traced back to the Middle Ages when guilds of craftsmen emerged, particularly among stonemasons who constructed cathedrals. These guilds provided not only a means of trade but also a framework for social and professional interaction.

Freemasonry as we know it today was officially founded in 1717 in London, when four existing lodges united to form the Grand Lodge of England. This marked the beginning of a movement that would rapidly spread throughout Europe and the American colonies. While Freemasonry is not a religion, it encourages members to believe in a Supreme Being, often referred to as the "Grand Architect of the Universe."

Freemasonry's organizational structure includes a hierarchy of degrees, with members progressing through a series of rites and rituals. This process of initiation involves elaborate ceremonies that convey moral and ethical lessons, often using allegorical symbols drawn from stonemasonry.

Influence on American History

The Freemasons played a pivotal role in shaping the ideological underpinnings of the United States. Many of the principles enshrined in the Declaration of Independence and the Constitution echo Masonic ideals, such as liberty, fraternity, and the pursuit of knowledge. The layout of Washington, D.C., including the positioning of key monuments, is believed to be influenced by Masonic symbolism and philosophy.

However, their secretive nature has led to suspicions and conspiracies throughout history. The Catholic Church has historically condemned Freemasonry, beginning in 1738, claiming it undermined religious authority and posed a threat to the faithful. In response, a significant anti-Masonic sentiment emerged in the United States, leading to the formation of the Anti-Masonic Party in the early 19th century.

Contemporary Freemasonry

The eye of providence is on the dollar bill.

Today, Freemasonry continues to exist, with millions of members worldwide. Their public image has been shaped significantly by the charitable work of groups like the Shriners, a Masonic subset known for its philanthropic efforts, including operating children's hospitals. Despite the transparency of their charity work, the mystique surrounding Freemasonry endures, with rumors of secret handshakes and hidden agendas perpetuating public curiosity.

The symbolism of Freemasonry, particularly the Square and Compasses, continues to captivate both supporters and critics. This symbol, often accompanied by the letter "G," has sparked debates regarding its meaning, with interpretations ranging from geometry to God.

3. The Illuminati

Origins and Ideological Foundations

Founded in Bavaria on May 1, 1776, by Adam Weishaupt, the Illuminati sought to promote Enlightenment ideals through reason and intellectual discourse. Frustrated by the oppressive influence of organized religion and the Bavarian monarchy, Weishaupt envisioned a society that would encourage critical thinking and the pursuit of knowledge. Drawing inspiration from the Enlightenment and other esoteric traditions, Weishaupt infiltrated Masonic lodges to recruit influential members of society, thereby establishing a network of powerful elites.

The organization was structured into three tiers, with members receiving classical nicknames and communicating in ciphers to maintain secrecy. The Illuminati attracted a diverse membership that included noblemen, intellectuals, and influential writers, allowing them to exert considerable influence over European society.

Suppression and Conspiracy Theories

Despite their initial success, the Illuminati faced significant opposition. In 1787, the Bavarian government, alarmed by the organization's growing influence, issued an edict banning secret societies, making membership in the Illuminati punishable by death. This crackdown effectively dismantled the organization, but the mythology surrounding the Illuminati did not die with it.

Conspiracy theories began to flourish, linking the Illuminati to significant historical events such as the French Revolution and the assassination of President John F. Kennedy. These theories posited that a shadowy elite was orchestrating world events from behind the scenes, manipulating political and social outcomes to create a "new world order."

The Modern Illumination

In contemporary discourse, the term "Illuminati" is often used to describe a vast array of secretive elites, from political leaders to celebrities. This notion reflects a deep-seated mistrust of power and governance, as individuals search for explanations for complex societal issues. While the original Illuminati no longer exists, the legacy of their ideas continues to inspire both admiration and fear, driving the narrative of secret societies in popular culture.

4. Skull and Bones

Origins at Yale University

Skull and Bones symbol

Founded in 1832 at Yale University, Skull and Bones is one of the most well-known secret societies in the United States. The society was established by William Huntington Russell, who was inspired by an occult society he encountered in Germany. His co-founder,

Alphonso Taft, would later become the Secretary of War under President Ulysses S. Grant and the father of President William Howard Taft, further embedding Skull and Bones into the fabric of American power.

Membership is limited to 15 seniors each year, known as "Bonesmen." Each initiation occurs within the confines of "The Tomb," the society's windowless meeting space, where members are sworn to secrecy. The rituals conducted within its walls remain largely undisclosed to the public, leading to speculation about the activities and oaths taken by members.

A Network of Influence

Skull and Bones boasts a membership list that includes several U.S. presidents, influential politicians, and business leaders. Notable members have included Presidents William Howard Taft, George H.W. Bush, and George W. Bush, as well as figures like John Kerry and Henry Luce, founder of Time magazine. This network of influence has led to claims that Skull and Bones operate with a "new world order" agenda, seeking to exert control over global affairs.

The society's emblem, a skull and crossbones, is accompanied by the number "322," which has been the subject of much speculation. One popular theory suggests that it refers to the year 322 B.C. when Alexander the Great died, hinting at a historical connection to power and mortality.

Conspiracy and Secrecy

The secretive nature of Skull and Bones has led to numerous conspiracy theories, particularly surrounding its supposed agenda to shape American and global policy. Critics argue that the society's exclusive membership and clandestine operations enable it to influence decisions that affect millions, operating outside the scrutiny of the public eye. The veil of secrecy surrounding society has led many to suspect that they are not merely a group of elite individuals but rather a shadowy cabal with ambitions to manipulate political landscapes and societal norms.

The 1986 exposé *America's Secret Establishment* by Anthony Sutton further fueled these conspiracy theories, claiming that Skull and Bones were intent on creating a new world order. Sutton argued that the society has a disproportionate influence on U.S. foreign and domestic policy, perpetuating a cycle of power that favors its members. This narrative has gained traction in popular culture, with references to Skull and Bones appearing in films, documentaries, and books, often framing it as an embodiment of elitism and secrecy.

The Modern-Day Skull and Bones

Despite the numerous conspiracy theories, the actual workings of Skull and Bones remain largely speculative. In recent years, there have been attempts to bring greater transparency to its operations, but the society's rituals and inner workings continue to be shrouded in mystery. The ongoing fascination with Skull and Bones reflects a broader societal obsession with secrecy and the influence of elite groups in shaping historical narratives.

5. The Bilderberg Group

Formation and Purpose

The 1966 Bilderberg conference in Wiesbaden, Germany. Top American and Europeans met, including NATO secretary general Manlio Brosio (left).

The Bilderberg Group was established in 1954 by Prince Bernhard of the Netherlands and a group of influential politicians, academics, and business leaders from North America and Europe. The inaugural meeting took place at the Hotel de Bilderberg in the Netherlands, and the group was created to foster dialogue and cooperation among Western powers amid growing anti-American sentiment in Europe during the Cold War.

Bilderberg meetings are held annually and involve a select group of around 120-140 attendees. While not strictly a secret society in the traditional sense, the Bilderberg Group operates under a level of confidentiality that has fueled speculation and conspiracy theories. The Chatham House Rule, which prevents participants from disclosing details of the discussions, adds to the group's aura of mystery.

High-Profile Attendees and Controversies

Attendees at Bilderberg meetings have included numerous influential figures, such as former U.S. Presidents Bill Clinton and George W. Bush, British Prime Ministers like Margaret Thatcher and Tony Blair, and prominent economists and financiers. This diverse membership highlights the group's focus on discussing significant global issues, such as economic policy, security, and international relations.

However, the closed-door nature of the meetings has given rise to numerous conspiracy theories, with critics alleging that the group is plotting a new world order or manipulating global events to serve the interests of the elite. These theories have gained traction in the age of social media, where the lack of transparency surrounding Bilderberg meetings is often cited as evidence of hidden agendas.

Addressing the Conspiracy

The Bilderberg Group has consistently denied allegations of conspiring to control world events, maintaining that their meetings serve as informal discussions on pressing global challenges. The group's official website states that participants attend as individuals rather than representing their governments or organizations, emphasizing the private nature of the meetings.

Despite this, the secrecy surrounding Bilderberg meetings continues to provoke public interest and skepticism. The group's perceived lack of accountability fuels a narrative that powerful individuals are operating behind the scenes, shaping the world without public oversight.

The Enduring Legacy of Secret Societies

The role of secret societies in shaping history is undeniable. From the Knights Templar to the Freemasons, Illuminati, Skull and Bones, and Bilderberg Group, these organizations have wielded considerable influence over political, social, and cultural landscapes. While many of the conspiracy theories surrounding these groups may lack concrete evidence, they reveal profound societal anxiety about power, secrecy, and control.

The enduring allure of secret societies lies in their ability to invoke curiosity and suspicion. They serve as symbols of the complexities of human governance and the intersection of power and secrecy. As we continue to unravel the mysteries of these organizations, it is essential to critically assess the narratives surrounding them, distinguishing between fact and fiction.

The history of secret societies is not merely a collection of intriguing anecdotes; it reflects deeper truths about the nature of authority and the human experience. Understanding these societies provides a lens through which we can analyze current events and the ongoing struggles for transparency, accountability, and justice in an increasingly complex global landscape.

In exploring the roles of secret societies, we uncover not only the hidden narratives of history but also the pervasive influence these groups have had in molding the present. The search for the truth about their impact is ongoing, and as we seek to illuminate these dark corners of our past, we must remain vigilant against the forces that seek to operate in secrecy, whether in ancient times or contemporary society.

As we close this chapter, remember that the allure of secret societies persists, drawing attention to the profound questions of power, secrecy, and the human experience. It is a reminder that history is not just about what is known; it is also about what remains hidden, waiting to be discovered.

Chapter 9: The Vatican's Hidden Archives

Vatican City

The Vatican. A name synonymous with religious power, ancient tradition, and… secrecy.

Within its imposing walls lies an endless amount of historical documents, artifacts, and texts, a collection so vast and valuable it's been dubbed "the memory of mankind." Yet, much of this collection remains hidden from public view, locked away in the Vatican Secret Archives.

This secrecy has fueled countless conspiracy theories and whispers of forbidden knowledge. Some claim the Vatican is hiding evidence of extraterrestrial contact, ancient advanced civilizations, or even the true origins of Christianity. Others believe the archives hold documents that could challenge the very foundations of the Church's power.

While some of these theories may be far-fetched, there's no denying that the Vatican Secret Archives holds a wealth of information that could rewrite our understanding of history. But why the secrecy? What is the Vatican so desperate to hide?

A Fortress of Knowledge

The Vatican Secret Archives, officially renamed the Vatican Apostolic Archives in 2019, are not your typical library.

Illustration of the Vatican Secret Archives reading room

This is a fortress of knowledge, spanning centuries and encompassing millions of documents, including papal bulls, correspondence with world leaders, and historical records dating back to the 8th century. Access to the archives is highly restricted. Only a select few scholars, vetted by the Vatican, are granted permission to study its contents. And even then, access is limited to specific documents and subject to strict conditions.

This exclusivity has led to accusations of censorship and suppression of information. Critics argue that the Vatican is selectively releasing information that supports its narrative while keeping anything controversial or potentially damaging under wraps.

The Secrets Within

While the full extent of the archives' contents remains unknown, glimpses into its hidden depths have revealed tantalizing hints of forbidden knowledge.

- **Ancient Texts:**

Ancient biblical manuscript

The Vatican possesses a vast collection of ancient texts, including early copies of the Bible, apocryphal gospels, and writings from ancient civilizations like Egypt and Mesopotamia. Some of these texts contain alternative versions of historical events or challenge traditional interpretations of religious doctrine.

- **Historical Records:**

Medieval papal bull

The archives hold detailed records of the Church's history, including its involvement in political intrigues, wars, and inquisitions. These records could shed light on dark chapters in the Church's past, such as its role in the Crusades or the persecution of heretics.

- **Scientific Discoveries:**

Depiction of the Historical Astronomical Chart

The Vatican has a long history of scientific inquiry, and its archives contain documents related to astronomy, mathematics, and medicine. Some speculate that the Vatican may possess knowledge of scientific discoveries that were suppressed for contradicting religious dogma.

- **Forbidden Artifacts:**

Depiction of the Ark of the Covenant

Rumors persist that the Vatican holds secret artifacts, such as the Ark of the Covenant or the Holy Grail. While the existence of such artifacts is debated, their presence in the archives would certainly explain the Vatican's desire for secrecy.

The Church's Narrative

The Vatican's official explanation for the secrecy surrounding its archives is that it's necessary to protect sensitive information and preserve the integrity of historical documents. However, critics argue that the real reason is to control the narrative and maintain the Church's power.

By selectively releasing information and suppressing anything that challenges its authority, the Vatican can shape public perception and maintain its image as a bastion of truth and morality.

The Power of Knowledge

The Vatican's control of knowledge has been a key factor in its historical influence. By acting as the gatekeeper of information, the Church could shape beliefs, influence political decisions, and maintain its dominance over the spiritual lives of millions.

But in the age of information, the Vatican's grip on knowledge is weakening. The internet and digital archives have made it increasingly difficult to control the flow of information. As more and more historical documents become accessible to the public, the Vatican's secrets are slowly being revealed.

The Vatican's Dilemma

The Vatican now faces a dilemma. On the one hand, it wants to maintain its image as a guardian of tradition and knowledge. On the other hand, it fears that greater transparency could expose uncomfortable truths and undermine its authority.

This tension is evident in the recent decision to open some sections of the archives to researchers. While this move has been welcomed by scholars, it's also seen as a calculated attempt to control the narrative and deflect criticism.

The Quest for Truth

The Vatican Secret Archives remains a source of fascination and frustration for historians, researchers, and anyone seeking to understand the hidden history of humanity. The secrets they hold could shed light on some of the greatest mysteries of our past, from the true origins of Christianity to the possibility of ancient advanced civilizations.

But the quest for truth is not easy. The Vatican's grip on knowledge is still strong, and its willingness to reveal its secrets remains limited. It will take a concerted effort by scholars, researchers, and the public to unlock the forbidden knowledge hidden within the Vatican's walls.

Controversial Documents and Artifacts

The Vatican Secret Archives, now officially known as the Vatican Apostolic Archives, houses a vast collection of documents and artifacts spanning centuries. Among these treasures are many controversial items that have fueled speculation and debate for centuries. Here are some of the most intriguing examples:

- **The Essene Gospel of Peace:**

  This alleged ancient Aramaic manuscript, discovered in 1923, is said to contain teachings of Jesus that differ significantly from those found in the canonical Gospels. The Vatican has never officially acknowledged the existence of this document, and its authenticity remains hotly debated.

- **The Donation of Constantine:**

  This document, dating from the 8th century, purports to be a decree by the Roman emperor Constantine the Great granting vast territories and privileges to the Pope. However, historians have long suspected that the document is a forgery, and the Vatican itself has admitted that its authenticity is uncertain.

- **The Galileo Affair:**

  The trial and condemnation of Galileo Galilei by the Catholic Church in 1633 is one of the most famous examples of the Church's conflict with science. The Vatican Archives contain extensive documentation of the trial, including Galileo's writings and transcripts of his interrogations. These documents offer valuable insights into the scientific and religious debates of the time.

- **The Third Secret of Fatima:**

  In 1917, three shepherd children in Fatima, Portugal, reported receiving visions of the Virgin Mary. The Virgin Mary is said to have revealed three secrets to the children, two of which have been made public. The third secret, however, remains hidden in the Vatican Archives. Some believe that the third secret contains a dire warning about the future of humanity, while others believe it is a fabrication.

- **The World's Largest Porn Collection:**

  One of the most bizarre rumors surrounding the Vatican Secret Archives is that it houses the world's largest collection of pornography. This rumor is based on the fact that the Vatican has a long history of collecting and preserving art, including some works that may be considered sexually explicit. However, there is no evidence to suggest that the Vatican possesses any such collection.

- **The Chinon Parchment:**
  This document, discovered in 2001, contains the minutes of the trial against the Knights Templar in 1308. The Knights Templar were a powerful military order accused of heresy and other crimes. The Chinon Parchment provides valuable insights into the order's history and the reasons for its dissolution.

- **The Gospel of Judas:**
  This controversial text, discovered in 1970, portrays Judas Iscariot in a more positive light than the traditional Christian narrative. The Vatican Secret Archives holds a

copy of this gospel, which has been the subject of much debate and speculation.

- **The Lost Library of Alexandria:**
  Some scholars believe that the Vatican Secret Archives may contain lost texts from the Library of Alexandria, one of the greatest libraries of antiquity. The library was destroyed in a fire in the 4th century AD, but some believe that copies of its scrolls may have been preserved by the Church.

- **The Gospel of Mary Magdalene:**

  This gnostic text portrays Mary Magdalene as a prominent disciple of Jesus, possibly even his closest confidante. It challenges the traditional view of her role and the early Church's hierarchy.

- **The Secret Book of John:** Another gnostic text, offers a different cosmological and theological perspective compared to the canonical gospels, including a more complex view of God and creation.
- **The Infancy Gospel of Thomas:**

  This apocryphal gospel describes the childhood of Jesus, portraying him as possessing miraculous powers even as a young boy.

- **The Book of Enoch:**

  Quoted in the Bible, but not included in the canon, this book describes fallen angels, the origins of demons, and apocalyptic prophecies.

Historical Documents:

1. The "Voynich Manuscript"

This enigmatic book, dating back to the 15th century, is filled with an unknown script and bizarre illustrations. Some believe it to be an alchemical text, others a coded message from a secret society, and still others an elaborate hoax. The Vatican's rumored possession of the manuscript fuels speculation that it holds the key to deciphering its secrets, perhaps revealing lost knowledge or heretical beliefs.

2. Records of the Inquisition

The Inquisition, a period of religious persecution lasting centuries, saw the Church ruthlessly suppress dissent and heresy. The archives are believed to contain detailed records of trials, interrogations, and executions. These documents could expose the brutal methods used by the Church to maintain its power and suppress alternative viewpoints, potentially damaging its image and challenging its moral authority.

3. Correspondence with Secret Societies

Throughout history, the Vatican has interacted with various secret societies, some with allegedly heretical or occult leanings. The archives may contain correspondence with groups like the Knights Templar, the Rosicrucians, or even the Illuminati. Such documents could reveal hidden alliances, power struggles, and the exchange of esoteric knowledge, potentially challenging the Church's public image and revealing its involvement in clandestine activities.

4. Ancient Maps and Diagrams

Some researchers believe the Vatican holds ancient maps and diagrams depicting lost continents, advanced technologies, or even extraterrestrial civilizations. These artifacts could challenge conventional history and reveal a past far more complex than we currently understand, potentially supporting alternative theories about human origins and the existence of advanced prehistoric cultures.

5. Forbidden Magical Texts

The Vatican has a long history of combating magic and witchcraft. However, it's also believed to possess a collection of grimoires and magical texts seized from accused practitioners. These texts could contain forbidden knowledge about rituals, spells, and occult practices, potentially revealing the Church's interest in the occult and its attempts to control and suppress magical traditions.

6. The "Index Librorum Prohibitorum"

This infamous list of banned books, maintained by the Church for centuries, included works deemed heretical, immoral, or dangerous to the faith. The archives likely hold copies of these banned books, offering a glimpse into the ideas and perspectives the Church sought to suppress. This could reveal a history of censorship and intellectual control, challenging the Church's claim to be a champion of truth and knowledge.

7. Documents Related to the "Black Pope"

The Superior General of the Society of Jesus, often referred to as the "Black Pope," is a powerful figure within the Church. The archives may contain documents related to the Black Pope's activities, including correspondence, reports, and internal memos. These documents could reveal the inner workings of the Jesuit order, its influence on Church policy, and its involvement in political and social affairs.

8. Artifacts from Ancient Pagan Religions

Before the rise of Christianity, Europe was home to a variety of pagan religions. The Vatican is believed to have collected and preserved artifacts from these religions, including idols, ritual objects, and sacred texts. These artifacts could offer valuable insights into pre-Christian beliefs and practices, potentially challenging the Church's narrative of its historical triumph and revealing the rich diversity of European spiritual traditions.

9. **The Papal Bull "Inter Caetera":** This 1493 document by Pope Alexander VI divided the newly discovered lands of the Americas between Spain and Portugal, laying the groundwork for colonization and the exploitation of indigenous peoples.

Artifacts:

- **The Spear of Destiny:**

Depiction of the Spear of Destiny

This legendary spear said to have pierced the side of Jesus during the crucifixion, is believed by some to possess supernatural powers.

- **The Shroud of Turin:**

This linen cloth, bearing the image of a man believed to be Jesus, has been a subject of intense debate for centuries. While the Vatican has not officially declared its authenticity, it remains a revered relic.

- **The "Vatican Necropolis":**

  Beneath St. Peter's Basilica lies a vast network of tombs and catacombs, rumored to contain the remains of early Christians and possibly even some of the Apostles.

The Vatican's Responsibility

The existence and significance of these documents and artifacts remain shrouded in mystery. The Vatican's reluctance to fully disclose its holdings raises questions about its commitment to transparency and its role in safeguarding historical truth.

The Vatican has a responsibility to make its archives accessible to scholars and the public. By doing so, it can contribute to a more complete understanding of human history and promote dialogue between faith and reason.

The continued secrecy surrounding the Vatican Secret Archives only serves to fuel speculation and distrust. It's time for the Vatican to embrace transparency and allow the world to see the full extent of its historical treasures.

Chapter 10: The Lost Libraries of the Ancient World: Unraveling the Truth Behind Atlantis

The legend of Atlantis has captivated human imagination for over two millennia. Originating from the works of the ancient Greek philosopher Plato, the tale of a powerful and advanced civilization that vanished beneath the waves has spurred countless debates among historians, archaeologists, and scholars. Is Atlantis merely a myth, an allegorical tale woven by Plato to convey philosophical ideas, or does it have roots in historical reality? This chapter delves deep into the origins of the Atlantis narrative, examining the evidence, the criticisms, and the enduring mystery that continues to fascinate us.

The Genesis of the Atlantis Story

Plato's dialogues, the **"Timaeus"** and the **"Critias,"** are the sole surviving accounts that detail the story of Atlantis. Written around 360 BCE, these works present a conversation between Socrates and his companions, wherein Critias recounts the tale of Atlantis—a mighty island nation that existed 9,000 years before their time.

According to Critias, the story was passed down through his family from his ancestor, Solon, a renowned Athenian statesman and one of the Seven Sages of Greece. Solon allegedly learned of Atlantis during his travels to Egypt, where priests at the Temple of Neith in Sais shared with him the ancient history inscribed on temple walls and pillars. These inscriptions told of a powerful empire beyond the Pillars of Hercules (modern-day Strait of Gibraltar) that had attempted to conquer Europe and Asia but was ultimately defeated by the ancient Athenians before succumbing to a cataclysmic disaster that submerged the island.

Plato's Intentions: Allegory or History?

A depiction of Plato's image

One of the central debates surrounding Atlantis is whether Plato intended the story as a historical account or merely as a fictional allegory to illustrate his philosophical ideas. Critics argue that the Atlantis narrative serves as a moral lesson on the dangers of hubris and the decline of moral values leading to societal downfall—a common theme in Plato's work.

However, a closer examination reveals significant differences between Atlantis and Plato's ideal society described in **"The Republic."** While Atlantis is depicted as a technologically advanced and materially wealthy civilization, it ultimately becomes morally corrupt, leading to its destruction. In contrast, Plato's ideal state is characterized by justice, virtue, and philosophical wisdom, governed by philosopher-kings. If Atlantis were merely a fictional representation of his ideal society, its portrayal as a doomed and morally bankrupt civilization seems contradictory.

Moreover, the level of detail provided about Atlantis's geography, culture, and politics suggests that Plato intended to convey more than an allegorical message. Descriptions of the island's concentric rings of land and water, its abundant resources, and the intricate laws governing its people imply a foundation in historical or at least traditional accounts.

Evidence Supporting Atlantis's Historical Basis

Consistency with Historical Knowledge

Plato's writings are remarkably accurate concerning other historical and geographical details. For instance, his mention of a sacred spring on the Acropolis once thought mythical, was corroborated by archaeological discoveries in the 20th century. Excavations revealed the remains of an ancient spring exactly where Plato had described, bolstering his credibility as a historian.

Furthermore, the political and social structures outlined in the Atlantis narrative reflect known practices of ancient civilizations. The division of the kingdom among ten kings, the hereditary monarchy constrained by laws, and the emphasis on maritime prowess align with historical models observed in ancient societies.

References in Other Ancient Texts

While Plato's account is the most comprehensive, there are hints of the Atlantis story in other ancient texts and traditions. The annual Panathenaea Festival in Athens established 125 years before Plato's birth, featured peplums (embroidered garments) depicting Athena's victory over the giants, which some interpretations suggest symbolize the defeat of Atlantis.

Additionally, other writers and philosophers of antiquity referenced Atlantis or similar stories. The historian **Diodorus Siculus** mentioned a large island in the Atlantic Ocean inhabited by a race that had conquered parts of Africa and Europe. **Proclus**, a Neoplatonist philosopher, cited earlier historians who affirmed the reality of Atlantis, including **Cratylus** and **Marcellus**, who purportedly had access to additional records.

The Egyptian Connection

A depiction of The Goddess Neth, Neith.

The credibility of the Atlantis narrative is further enhanced by its Egyptian origins. The priests of Sais, who conveyed the story to Solon, claimed that their civilization had records of ancient events far predating Greek history. Egypt's long-standing tradition of recording history on temple walls and papyri lends weight to the possibility that the story of Atlantis was preserved through generations.

The Temple of Neith in Sais, where Solon supposedly learned of Atlantis, was dedicated to the goddess Neith—a deity associated with creation, wisdom, and warfare. The association of Atlantis with Neith underscores the gravity and authenticity the Egyptians might have attributed to the tale.

Criticisms and Counterarguments

Despite these supporting elements, skepticism about the historical existence of Atlantis persists. Critics often cite several key arguments against its reality.

Lack of Archaeological Evidence

Perhaps the most significant challenge to the Atlantis narrative is the absence of concrete archaeological evidence. No definitive remnants of such an advanced civilization have been discovered in the Atlantic Ocean or elsewhere that match Plato's description. While underwater explorations have uncovered intriguing structures, none have been conclusively linked to Atlantis.

Chronological Discrepancies

Plato places the destruction of Atlantis 9,000 years before Solon's time, which would be around 9,600 BCE. This predates known advanced civilizations by several millennia, leading some scholars to suggest that the timeline is exaggerated or symbolic. The possibility of a mistranslation or misinterpretation of the Egyptian numerical system (confusing hundreds with thousands) has been proposed, which could adjust the timeline to a more plausible historical period.

Allegorical Interpretation

As previously mentioned, many scholars view the Atlantis story as an allegory. They argue that Plato used the narrative to critique the moral decay he perceived in Athens and to emphasize his philosophical ideas about ideal governance and societal structures. The detailed descriptions could be a literary device to lend authenticity to his message.

Alternative Theories and Locations

Over the centuries, numerous theories have emerged proposing various locations for Atlantis, each attempting to align the legend with known historical events or geographical features.

The Minoan Civilization and Thera (Santorini)

One popular theory suggests that the Minoan civilization on Crete and the nearby island of Thera (modern-day Santorini) inspired the Atlantis story. The Minoans were a technologically advanced society with impressive architecture, extensive trade networks, and a powerful navy.

Around 1600 BCE, the volcanic eruption on Thera devastated the region, leading to the decline of the Minoan civilization. Proponents argue that this cataclysm mirrors the destruction of Atlantis described by Plato. However, significant discrepancies exist, including differences in chronology, geography, and cultural details.

The Atlantic Ocean Hypothesis

Some researchers hold that Atlantis was indeed located in the Atlantic Ocean, possibly near the Azores or the submerged island of Spartel near the Strait of Gibraltar. Geological studies have identified areas where landmasses could have existed during the last Ice Age when sea levels were lower.

However, the challenges of deep-sea archaeology and the vastness of the ocean make it difficult to gather definitive evidence supporting this theory.

Other Proposed Locations

Various other locations have been proposed, including:

- **Antarctica:** Based on shifts in Earth's crust and maps like the Piri Reis map showing ice-free coastlines.
- **South America:** Citing similarities between Andean civilizations and Plato's descriptions.

- **The Caribbean:** Suggesting remnants of Atlantis could be found among the submerged structures near Bimini.

Each theory attempts to reconcile Plato's account with geological and historical data, but none have achieved widespread acceptance.

The Enduring Legacy of Atlantis

Regardless of its historical veracity, the story of Atlantis has had a profound impact on culture and thought throughout history.

Influence on Exploration

The legend of Atlantis fueled the imagination of explorers during the Age of Discovery. Christopher Columbus and other navigators were intrigued by tales of lands beyond the known world, potentially inspired by ancient accounts like Plato's.

Cultural and Artistic Depictions

Atlantis has been a rich source of inspiration for literature, art, and entertainment. From Francis Bacon's "New Atlantis" to modern films and novels, the allure of a lost civilization continues to captivate audiences.

Symbolism and Philosophical Implications

Atlantis serves as a cautionary tale about the dangers of moral decay and the hubris of societies that overreach. It prompts reflection on the cyclical nature of civilizations—their rise, peak, and eventual decline—and the factors that contribute to their downfall.

Re-examining Atlantis in Light of Modern Discoveries

Advancements in archaeology, geology, and technology have opened new avenues for exploring ancient mysteries. Underwater archaeology, in particular, has the potential to uncover submerged sites that could shed light on lost civilizations.

Göbekli Tepe and Revision of History

Göbeklitepe

The discovery of Göbekli Tepe in southeastern Turkey, dated to around 9,600 BCE—the same period Plato assigns to Atlantis—has challenged conventional timelines of human civilization. This archaeological site features monumental architecture predating the advent of agriculture and established settlements, suggesting that complex societies may have existed earlier than previously thought.

Rising Sea Levels and Submerged Settlements

The end of the last Ice Age saw significant rises in sea levels, inundating coastal areas and potentially obliterating evidence of ancient societies. Submerged settlements have been discovered off the coasts of India, Japan, and other regions, indicating that much of human history may lie beneath the oceans.

The Role of Catastrophic Events

Research into past catastrophic events, such as comet impacts, massive volcanic eruptions, and sudden climate shifts, supports the idea that advanced societies could have been disrupted or destroyed. The Younger Dryas Impact Hypothesis, for example, proposes that a comet impact around 10,800 BCE led to sudden cooling and widespread extinctions.

The Case for a Reassessment

Given the accumulation of new evidence and the reevaluation of ancient timelines, it is prudent to revisit the Atlantis narrative with an open mind. Dismissing the story outright overlooks the possibility that it contains kernels of historical truth, preserved through oral traditions and myth.

Oral Traditions as Historical Records

In many cultures, oral traditions serve as vital repositories of history, especially in the absence of written records. Myths and legends often encode real events, places, and experiences, albeit embellished or altered over time. Recognizing this, historians and archaeologists increasingly consider indigenous narratives when reconstructing the past.

Interdisciplinary Approaches

A comprehensive investigation into the Atlantis story benefits from an interdisciplinary approach, integrating insights from:

- **Archaeology:** Examining material evidence of ancient societies.
- **Geology:** Understanding Earth's changes that could have impacted civilizations.
- **Anthropology:** Studying human cultures and their development.
- **Mythology and Comparative Religion:** Analyzing common themes and narratives across different cultures.

By bridging these disciplines, researchers can construct a more nuanced understanding of ancient history.

The legend of Atlantis occupies a unique space at the intersection of history, myth, and philosophy. While definitive proof of its existence remains elusive, the enduring fascination with this lost civilization underscores a fundamental human curiosity about our origins and the forces that shape societies.

Atlantis challenges us to question established narratives, to consider the possibility of forgotten chapters in human history, and to recognize the fragility of civilizations in the face of natural and self-inflicted catastrophes. Whether Atlantis was a real place or a masterful allegory, its impact on our collective consciousness is undeniable, and its lessons remain relevant to this day.

Chapter 11: Unveiling Suppressed Scientific Discoveries—the Hidden Fauna of the Red Sea Islands

Scientific discovery has always been a cornerstone of human progress, expanding our understanding of the world and informing our stewardship of it. However, throughout history, various factors have led to the suppression or neglect of significant scientific findings. This chapter delves into the intriguing case of the Red Sea islands' non-volant terrestrial mammalian fauna—a subject that has remained largely obscure due to a combination of geopolitical instability, environmental challenges, and scientific oversight.

We explore how the unique biodiversity of the Red Sea islands has been underreported and underexplored, leading to a gap in our knowledge that has significant implications for conservation and ecological understanding. By examining the available records, recent discoveries, and the factors contributing to the suppression of scientific discoveries in this region, we aim to highlight the importance of renewed scientific attention and the potential benefits it holds for biodiversity conservation.

The Importance of Scientific Discovery and Its Suppression

Scientific discovery drives innovation, informs policy, and enhances our comprehension of the natural world. However, the suppression of scientific findings—whether intentional or unintentional—can hinder progress, obscure truths, and negatively impact environmental conservation efforts. Suppression can occur due to political agendas, economic interests, lack of funding, or simply neglect due to perceived insignificance.

In the context of biodiversity, suppressed or overlooked discoveries can lead to the loss of species before they are even documented, impeding our ability to protect and preserve ecosystems. The Red Sea islands present a compelling case where a combination of factors has led to the underrepresentation of scientific knowledge about their terrestrial mammalian fauna.

The Red Sea: A Region Rich in Biodiversity and History

Realistic satellite-style illustrations of the Red Sea

The Red Sea is a narrow, elongated body of water separating the eastern coast of North Africa from the western Arabian Peninsula. It is globally significant for its unique marine biodiversity, hosting some of the world's most pristine coral reefs and a plethora of marine species, many of which are endemic.

Geographically, the Red Sea occupies a substantial part of the submerged Afro-Syrian Great Rift Valley. It is characterized by long, straight shorelines and narrow coastal plains, with a maximum width of approximately 355 kilometers. The sea is connected to the Mediterranean via the Suez Canal to the north and the Indian Ocean through the Bab el Mandeb Strait to the south.

The Red Sea islands, numbering over 350 in Eritrea alone and more than 100 in Yemen, are diverse in their geological origins. Some are volcanic, such as those in the Zubayr and Hanish archipelagos, while others are low, flat, and sandy, composed of fossilized coral. Historically, during the Last Glacial Maximum, many of these islands were connected to the mainland, facilitating faunal exchanges.

Despite the richness of marine life, the terrestrial biodiversity of the Red Sea islands is comparatively poor. The harsh climatic conditions, lack of freshwater sources, and limited vegetation have contributed to a depauperate terrestrial fauna, primarily composed of species also found on the mainland.

The Terrestrial Mammalian Fauna of the Red Sea Islands

An Overview of Findings

A comprehensive review of the non-volant (non-flying) terrestrial mammals of the Red Sea islands reveals a surprisingly limited fauna. The composition is oligotypic, consisting of only a few taxa, mostly anthropochorous species (those spread by human activity), shared with the mainland of eastern Africa and western Arabia. These species are repeated monotonously on the few islands inhabited by mammals.

Notably, there are no endemic terrestrial mammalian species identified on the Red Sea islands. The only endemic vertebrates are three species of snakes and, possibly, one gazelle (Gazella arabica), although its status remains enigmatic.

Species Composition

The mammalian fauna includes:

- **Carnivores**: The white-tailed mongoose (Ichneumia albicauda), an unidentified fox species, and possibly the striped hyena (Hyaena hyaena).
- **Rodents**: Four species commensal with humans, including the black rat (Rattus rattus), the house mouse (Mus musculus), the Eastern spiny mouse (Acomys dimidiatus), and the Northeast African spiny mouse (Acomys cahirinus).
- **Shrews**: The Sahelian shrew (Crocidura pasha) and the Asian house shrew (Suncus murinus).
- **Ungulates**: Gazelles of the genus Gazella and Nanger, specifically the mountain gazelle (Gazella gazella), the Dorcas gazelle (Gazella dorcas), and Soemmerring's gazelle (Nanger soemmerringii).

Lack of Endemism and Possible Explanations

The absence of endemic mammals can be attributed to several factors:

1. **Recent Connection with the Mainland**: During the Last Glacial Maximum, many islands were connected to the mainland due to lower sea levels, allowing terrestrial fauna to migrate freely.
2. **Harsh Climatic Conditions**: The arid environment, scarcity of freshwater, and limited vegetation make survival challenging for many species.
3. **Human Influence**: Human activities, such as the deliberate introduction of species for hunting or the accidental introduction of commensal species, have shaped the current fauna.

Human-Mediated Introductions

Humans have a long history of interaction with the Red Sea islands, dating back to prehistoric times. Evidence suggests that gazelles and other species were introduced to some islands for hunting purposes or as a food source. The white-tailed mongoose may have been introduced to control rodent populations or inadvertently through human settlement.

Challenges to Scientific Research in the Red Sea Islands

Geopolitical Instability

Political instability and conflict in the countries bordering the Red Sea, such as Eritrea, Sudan, Yemen, and Saudi Arabia, have hindered scientific exploration. Safety concerns and access restrictions have made it difficult for researchers to conduct fieldwork, leading to gaps in data and understanding.

Accessibility and Environmental Conditions

Many of the islands are remote, with no freshwater sources, making prolonged stays challenging. The harsh climate, characterized by extreme heat and aridity, adds to the difficulty of conducting research. These conditions have deterred extensive scientific study and contributed to the suppression of potential discoveries.

Lack of Funding and Resources

Scientific research in these regions often suffers from a lack of funding, equipment, and institutional support. Priorities may be directed towards more accessible or immediately pressing issues, leaving the biodiversity of the Red Sea islands underexplored.

Historical Accounts and Misinterpretations

Historical records of the fauna on the Red Sea islands are scattered and sometimes inconsistent. Early explorers and naturalists, such as Bruce of Kinnaird (1790), Henry Salt, and Eduard Rüppell, provided some of the first accounts of gazelles and other mammals on the islands. However, these records often lacked precise locations or detailed descriptions, leading to confusion and misinterpretation.

For instance, reports of the striped hyena and an unidentified fox species on islands like Debir and Sumayr are based on anecdotal evidence or misidentified specimens. The presence of the hamadryas baboon (Papio hamadryas) in Massawa and Farasan Al-Kebir is likely due to human introduction, possibly as pets, rather than natural populations.

Such misinterpretations have contributed to an unclear understanding of the islands' fauna and have obscured the true nature of their biodiversity.

The Role of Human Activity in the Distribution of Fauna

Human activities have significantly influenced the distribution and composition of terrestrial mammals on the Red Sea islands.

Gazelles were likely introduced to islands like Dahlak Kebir and the Farasan archipelago for hunting and as a food source. The practice of releasing ungulates on islands as a form of game management has historical precedence in the region.

Commensal rodents, such as the black rat and house mouse, have been inadvertently introduced through maritime trade and human settlement. These species often have detrimental effects on native fauna, particularly ground-nesting birds, through predation and competition.

Impact on Endemic Species

The introduction of predators like the white-tailed mongoose has had adverse effects on local wildlife. On the Farasan archipelago, mongooses have been linked to the decline of ground-nesting seabirds and the breeding success of species like the osprey.

Suppression and Neglect of Scientific Discoveries in the Red Sea Region

The combination of challenging research conditions, geopolitical instability, and misinterpretations has led to the suppression and neglect of significant scientific discoveries in the Red Sea region.

Underrepresentation in Scientific Literature

The mammals of the Red Sea islands are underrepresented in scientific literature. Data on species presence, distribution, and ecology are sparse and scattered across obscure or outdated publications. This underrepresentation perpetuates a cycle of neglect, where the lack of information leads to diminished interest and further suppression of research.

Loss of Specimens and Data

Specimens collected during early expeditions are often poorly preserved or mislabeled, leading to confusion in species identification. For example, the enigmatic status of Gazella arabica is compounded by the fact that the type specimen consists of a skull and skin from different individuals, possibly from different locations.

Overlooked Biodiversity

The lack of comprehensive surveys means that potentially significant findings remain undiscovered. The possibility of endemic species existing on unexplored islands cannot be ruled out. However, without dedicated research efforts, these species may remain unknown, and any conservation needs unaddressed.

The Impact of Suppression on Biodiversity Conservation

Suppression and neglect of scientific discoveries have direct implications for biodiversity conservation.

Inadequate Conservation Measures

Without accurate data on species presence and population status, conservation measures cannot be effectively implemented. Species may decline or become extinct without notice, especially on islands where ecosystems are fragile and species have limited ranges.

Failure to Recognize Endemic Species

Potentially endemic species may go unrecognized due to lack of research. Endemism is a crucial factor in conservation prioritization. Failure to identify endemic species means they receive no specific protection, increasing their vulnerability.

Invasive Species Management

Understanding the impact of introduced species is essential for managing invasive populations and protecting native fauna. Suppression of research hinders the development of effective management strategies.

Unveiling the Hidden Fauna: Recent Discoveries and Their Significance

Despite the challenges, recent efforts have begun to shed light on the terrestrial mammals of the Red Sea islands.

New Records and Species Identification

- **Northeast African Spiny Mouse (Acomys cahirinus)**: Collected in the Dahlak archipelago, this species adds to the known rodent fauna of the islands.
- **Undetermined Shrew (Crocidura sp.)**: A skull found on Isratu Island indicates the presence of a shrew species yet to be identified.
- **White-tailed Mongoose (Ichneumia albicauda)**: Recorded on Dissei and Farasan Al-Kebir, highlighting the species' adaptability and potential human-mediated introduction.

Genetic Studies and Taxonomic Clarifications

Advancements in genetic analysis have allowed for better taxonomic clarification of species like the gazelles on Dahlak Kebir and the Farasan archipelago. For example, genetic studies suggest that the gazelles on Dahlak Kebir are a dwarf variant of Soemmerring's gazelle, possibly due to insular dwarfism.

Similarly, the enigmatic Gazella arabica has been the subject of genetic scrutiny, revealing that the skin and skull of the type specimen may belong to different species, thus clarifying its taxonomic status.

Significance for Conservation and Ecology

These discoveries have significant implications:

- **Biodiversity Assessment**: They contribute to a more accurate assessment of the islands' biodiversity.
- **Conservation Prioritization**: Identifying species and understanding their status informs conservation priorities and strategies.
- **Ecological Understanding**: Insights into species adaptations, such as insular dwarfism, enhance our understanding of evolutionary processes in isolated environments.

The Need for Renewed Scientific Exploration

The case of the Red Sea islands underscores the need for renewed scientific exploration and attention.

Comprehensive surveys and studies are necessary to fill the existing knowledge gaps. This includes systematic documentation of species, population assessments, and ecological studies to understand species interactions and environmental pressures.

Collaborative Efforts

International collaboration can help overcome some of the challenges posed by geopolitical instability and resource limitations. Partnerships between local authorities, international organizations, and researchers can facilitate access and provide necessary support.

Incorporating local and traditional knowledge can enhance scientific understanding. Local communities may have observations and insights that can inform research and conservation efforts.

Emphasizing Conservation

Highlighting the unique aspects of the Red Sea islands can attract attention to their conservation needs. Recognizing the potential for endemic species and the ecological significance of the islands can drive conservation initiatives.

The Red Sea islands serve as a poignant example of how challenging conditions, misinterpretations, and oversight can lead to significant gaps in scientific knowledge.

By unveiling the hidden fauna of the Red Sea islands and highlighting the factors contributing to their obscurity, we emphasize the importance of vigilance in scientific exploration. Recognizing suppression allows us to address it proactively, ensuring that discoveries are not lost and that biodiversity is adequately documented and protected.

Renewed scientific attention to the Red Sea islands holds the promise of uncovering new species, understanding unique ecological processes, and informing conservation efforts that can preserve these fragile ecosystems for future generations.

Chapter 12: Unveiling the Hidden Voices of World War II

History is often written by the victors, but what happens when pivotal stories are buried, overlooked, or intentionally suppressed? The conventional narratives of World War II have been etched into our collective consciousness—epic battles, heroic soldiers, and tyrannical leaders. Yet, beneath the surface lies an untold story that challenges our understanding of propaganda, resistance, and the very nature of warfare. This is the story of the German-speaking Jewish refugees who, after fleeing Nazi persecution, became the unexpected soldiers of psychological warfare within the British Broadcasting Corporation (BBC).

These refugees, once celebrated artists, journalists, and intellectuals in their homelands, found themselves in exile, stripped of their identities and professional platforms. But in a twist of fate, it was precisely their deep understanding of German culture, language, and society that positioned them as formidable assets in the fight against the Third Reich. Operating from the heart of London, they crafted radio programs that penetrated the ironclad propaganda of Joseph Goebbels, sowing seeds of doubt and dissent within Nazi Germany.

This chapter exposes the tricky web of contradictions, sacrifices, and moral dilemmas faced by these unlikely warriors. It delves into how their contributions were both a weapon against tyranny and a personal struggle against the very ideologies that had cast them out. Moreover, it confronts the unsettling reality of how their stories have been marginalized in historical accounts, and overshadowed by broader wartime narratives.

Prepare to journey into the clandestine operations of the BBC's German Service during World War II—a realm where exiled Jews became the voice of British propaganda, challenging the Nazi regime from afar while grappling with their own identities. This is not just a tale of war; it's a revelation of suppressed histories that demands recognition and reexamination.

The Birth of a Silent Army

When Adolf Hitler rose to power in 1933, the landscape of Europe began to shift dramatically. Among the first to feel the oppressive weight of Nazi policies were the Jewish communities of Germany and its annexed territories. Intellectuals, artists, and professionals were systematically stripped of their rights, livelihoods, and, ultimately, their citizenship. The exodus of German-speaking Jews began—a flood of refugees seeking safety in countries like England.

By the outbreak of World War II, approximately 80,000 Jewish refugees from Germany, Austria, and Czechoslovakia had found their way to British shores. Among them were seasoned journalists, playwrights, actors, and scholars who had once been integral to the cultural fabric of Central Europe. In their new homeland, they faced not only the challenges of displacement but also suspicion and alienation, often categorized as "enemy aliens" due to their nationality.

Yet, as Britain braced itself against the Nazi onslaught, the need for effective propaganda became paramount. The British government recognized that to undermine the Nazi regime, they needed to reach the German people directly. Radio waves became the new battleground, and the BBC's German Service was established as a critical weapon in psychological warfare.

But who could better understand and communicate with the German populace than those who had lived among them? The exiled German-speaking Jews possessed an unparalleled familiarity with the nuances of German society, culture, and language. Despite the irony and bitter paradox, these refugees were enlisted to craft the very messages that would challenge the regime responsible for their persecution.

The BBC's Secret Weapon: Refugee Talent

The BBC's German Service was not just another broadcasting department; it was a strategic hub designed to penetrate the formidable Nazi propaganda machine. From the outset, British officials understood that traditional methods would be insufficient. They needed voices that could resonate authentically with German listeners, voices that carried the credibility and intimacy necessary to foster doubt about the Nazi regime.

Enter individuals like Martin Miller, born Rudolf Müller in Moravia, who had been a prominent actor in Vienna and Berlin. Forced into exile due to his Jewish heritage, Miller found himself in London, initially scraping by with odd jobs. His unique talent for mimicking Adolf Hitler's voice and mannerisms caught the attention of the BBC, and soon he was delivering satirical speeches that aired directly into Germany. Posing as Hitler, he subverted the Führer's messages, injecting humor and absurdity to erode the infallible image the Nazis cultivated.

Similarly, Annemarie Hase, a celebrated cabaret performer from Berlin, became the voice of "Frau Wernicke," a fictional German housewife who offered candid monologues criticizing the hardships and absurdities of life under Nazi rule. Her character spoke in the authentic Berlin dialect, connecting with everyday Germans in a way that no foreign broadcaster could.

These refugees, along with many others, became the backbone of the BBC's German Service. They wrote scripts, performed sketches, and developed programs that blended news, entertainment, and subversive commentary. Their work was not merely about disseminating information; it was about psychological infiltration—challenging Nazi narratives from within and fostering a sense of disillusionment among German citizens and soldiers.

Navigating a Maze of Contradictions

While the contributions of these refugees were invaluable, their positions were fraught with contradictions and moral complexities. On one hand, they were essential to Britain's war effort, utilizing their expertise to fight against the regime that had sought their destruction. On the other, they were operating in a society that often viewed them with suspicion due to their German origins.

The British government's policies towards "enemy aliens" placed severe restrictions on their movements and freedoms. Many refugees faced curfews, travel limitations, and even internment. The very individuals who were producing propaganda for the BBC were simultaneously subjected to the indignities of mistrust by their host nation.

Furthermore, the BBC itself grappled with concerns about the refugees' influence on their programming. Officials worried that German listeners would dismiss broadcasts if they suspected they were produced by Jews or exiled Germans, whom Nazi propaganda had demonized. This led to a paradoxical situation where the BBC relied on the refugees' talents but often kept their identities hidden, denying them recognition and perpetuating a sense of otherness.

These tensions extended into content decisions as well. The BBC was cautious about addressing Jewish persecution directly, fearing it would alienate German listeners. This meant that the refugees, many of whom had lost family and friends to the Holocaust, had to suppress their grievances and focus on broader anti-Nazi messaging.

The Power of Satire and Subversion

In the realm of propaganda, humor, and satire emerged as potent tools. They allowed broadcasters to critique the Nazi regime indirectly, bypassing censorship and resonating with listeners fatigued by war and propaganda. The refugees harnessed their artistic backgrounds to create compelling characters and narratives that reflected the realities of German life under Nazism.

Frau Wernicke: The Voice of the People

Annemarie Hase's portrayal of Frau Wernicke became one of the BBC's most successful propaganda efforts. The character was a sharp-tongued, no-nonsense Berlin housewife who spoke candidly about the struggles of daily life—food shortages, air raids, and the hypocrisy of Nazi officials. Through her monologues, written by Bruno Adler, another Jewish refugee and former Bauhaus lecturer, Frau Wernicke highlighted the growing discontent among ordinary Germans.

The authenticity of her dialect and the relatable nature of her grievances made Frau Wernicke a beloved figure among listeners. She didn't overtly denounce the regime but used irony and common-sense observations to undermine its authority. Her popularity was such that Nazi officials reportedly became concerned about her influence, despite the broadcasts being illegal to listen to.

Lance-Corporal Adolf Hirnschal: A Soldier's Perspective

Another notable creation was "Die Briefe des Gefreiten Adolf Hirnschal" (The Letters of Lance-Corporal Adolf Hirnschal), penned by Robert Lucas, born Robert Ehrenzweig, a Viennese writer and journalist. Through fictional letters to his wife, Hirnschal, voiced by Fritz Schrecker, conveyed the grim realities and absurdities faced by German soldiers on the front lines.

Hirnschal was portrayed as an everyman—naïve, and loyal, yet increasingly disillusioned by the war's futility and the incompetence of his superiors. The character's humor and honesty offered a stark contrast to the glorified depictions of war propagated by Nazi media. His letters subtly encouraged soldiers and their families to question the purpose and conduct of the war.

These programs were not mere entertainment; they were carefully crafted psychological operations. By humanizing the struggles of German citizens and soldiers, they fostered empathy and opened channels for critical thought, all while avoiding overt propaganda that could trigger immediate dismissal or backlash.

The Irony of Recognition and Anonymity

Despite the success of these programs, the refugees behind them remained largely anonymous. The BBC's policy was to keep their identities concealed to protect them from Nazi retaliation and to maintain the credibility of the broadcasts. However, this anonymity also meant that their sacrifices and contributions went unacknowledged.

The fear of anti-Semitic reactions led the BBC to downplay or avoid Jewish themes in their programming. Even as reports of the Holocaust emerged, the corporation hesitated to address them directly, concerned that such content would be counterproductive. This left the refugee broadcasters in a painful position—using their talents to fight against the regime that was annihilating their people, yet unable to speak openly about the atrocities.

Furthermore, within the BBC and British society, latent prejudices and suspicions persisted. Some officials expressed concerns about the "Jewishness" of voices and content, fearing it would undermine their efforts. The refugees were thus caught between being indispensable assets and being viewed as potential liabilities.

Post-War Realities and Continued Marginalization

When the war ended, one might expect that the refugees' contributions would be celebrated and that they would find acceptance in their adopted homeland. Instead, many faced ongoing challenges. The BBC began to shift its focus towards rebuilding relationships with the German population, and there was a push to hire native Germans who had remained in the country during the war.

This transition often came at the expense of the refugees who had served faithfully. Some were let go or demoted, and their positions were given to individuals perceived as better suited for peacetime broadcasting. The irony was stark—the very people who had fought against Nazism were being sidelined in favor of those who had lived under it.

Moreover, the refugees continued to grapple with their identities. They were neither fully British nor could they return to their homelands, now scarred by war and genocide. Their stories remained overshadowed, their experiences compartmentalized and often ignored in the broader narratives of the war and its aftermath.

The Suppression and Neglect of Their Legacy

The historical record has not been kind to these unsung heroes. Their contributions have been largely omitted from mainstream accounts of World War II. Several factors have contributed to this neglect:

1. **Political Expediency**: In the post-war period, as Cold War tensions escalated, Western powers were eager to integrate West Germany into the fold against the Soviet Union. This necessitated a certain amnesia about the recent past, including the complexities of German complicity and resistance.
2. **Cultural Prejudices**: Anti-Semitism did not disappear with the fall of the Third Reich. Prejudices persisted in subtle and overt ways, influencing whose stories were told and valued.
3. **Personal Anonymity**: The enforced anonymity during the war meant that the refugees' identities and stories were not documented or celebrated. Without public recognition, their narratives were easily lost.
4. **Complex Identities**: The refugees occupied a liminal space—German by birth but rejected by their homeland, Jewish but often secular and assimilated, and British

residents but not fully accepted. This complexity did not fit neatly into post-war historical frameworks.

5. **Overshadowed by Larger Narratives**: The enormity of the Holocaust and the focus on military strategies and political leaders in historical accounts left little room for the nuanced stories of individual contributors to the war effort.

The Imperative to Acknowledge and Remember

Uncovering the stories of these refugee broadcasters is not merely an academic exercise; it is a moral imperative. Recognizing their contributions challenges us to rethink the narratives we accept and the histories we preserve. It sheds light on the multifaceted nature of resistance against tyranny and the personal sacrifices made by those caught in the crossfire of global conflict.

Their experiences also offer valuable lessons for contemporary society:

- **The Power of Cultural Intelligence**: The refugees' deep understanding of German culture was instrumental in crafting effective propaganda. This underscores the importance of cultural and linguistic expertise in international relations and conflict resolution.
- **The Consequences of Prejudice**: The suspicion and marginalization they faced, even while serving the British war effort, highlight how prejudices can undermine unity and justice, even among allies.
- **The Complexity of Identity**: Their stories illustrate the challenges faced by displaced individuals who navigate multiple identities, a reality that remains pertinent in today's globalized world with ongoing refugee crises.
- **The Need for Inclusive Histories**: By bringing these hidden narratives to light, we enrich our understanding of the past and ensure that contributions from all backgrounds are valued and remembered.

Reclaiming Their Voices

In recent years, there has been a gradual resurgence of interest in the stories of these refugee broadcasters. Scholars, journalists, and descendants have begun to piece together their histories, drawing from archives, personal letters, and surviving recordings.

Books and documentaries have emerged, shedding light on figures like Robert Lucas and his creation of Adolf Hirnschal, or the enduring legacy of Frau Wernicke. These efforts are not just about honoring the past but also about informing the present—recognizing the enduring impact of propaganda, the importance of media in shaping public opinion, and how marginalized individuals can influence the course of history.

Moreover, these stories resonate with current discussions about refugees, immigration, and the value of diverse perspectives in society. They serve as a reminder that those who are cast out can become critical contributors to their new communities if given the opportunity and recognition.

The untold story of the German-speaking Jewish refugees who became the voice of British propaganda during World War II is a testament to resilience, ingenuity, and the complexities of human identity. Their experiences challenge us to confront uncomfortable truths about prejudice, the selective nature of historical memory, and how valuable contributions can be overlooked or suppressed.

As we reflect on this hidden chapter of history, it becomes clear that our understanding of the past is incomplete without acknowledging the roles played by those who operated in the shadows. By bringing their stories to the forefront, we not only honor their sacrifices but also enrich our comprehension of the forces that shaped the modern world.

It is incumbent upon us to ensure that such narratives are not forgotten—that the voices of the displaced, the marginalized, and the silenced are heard and integrated into the fabric of history. Only then can we claim to have a true and comprehensive understanding of our past, and perhaps, forge a more just and inclusive future.

The journey into the hidden facets of World War II does not end here. The stories of these refugee broadcasters are intertwined with broader themes of censorship, propaganda, and the manipulation of information—issues that continue to resonate today. As we move forward, let us remain vigilant in uncovering and acknowledging the suppressed histories that shape our world.

Part III: The Unexplained and the Paranormal

In the upcoming pages, we'll dive headfirst into the fascinating realms of UFOs and extraterrestrial beings, exploring the tantalizing possibility that we are not alone in the universe and perhaps have never been. We'll unravel the secrets of ancient civilizations like Atlantis and Lemuria, delving into legends of advanced societies that vanished without a trace but may have left behind clues to their extraordinary existence.

As we voyage further, we'll unlock the mysteries of our planetary neighborhood, uncovering astonishing facts and theories about the celestial bodies that share our solar system. Could there be hidden histories etched into the very fabric of these planets, waiting for us to decipher? We'll also delve into the depths of forbidden Paleolithic history, unearthing evidence that suggests humanity's story is far older and more complex than conventional wisdom admits. Imagine discovering artifacts and knowledge that rewrite the timelines of human evolution!

Finally, we'll immerse ourselves in the rich fabrics of the Indian and Chinese mystery, exploring ancient texts, enigmatic structures, and spiritual insights that have intrigued scholars and adventurers alike for centuries. From the mystical powers of forgotten sages to the unexplained phenomena that defy logic, this exploration promises to be as enlightening as it is thrilling.

So, fasten your seatbelts and prepare your minds for a whirlwind tour through the unexplained, the mysterious, and the downright mind-boggling. This is not just a read—it's an adventure into the unknown that will leave you questioning the very foundations of history and eager for more. The truth is out there, and together, we're going to find it!

Chapter 13: UFOs and Extraterrestrial Intervention

For centuries, we've gazed upward, pondering whether we are truly alone in this universe or if other intelligent beings share this celestial stage with us. The possibility of extraterrestrial life isn't just a topic for science fiction enthusiasts; it's a profound question that touches the very essence of our existence. In recent decades, this quest for answers has taken on an urgent tone, fueled by tantalizing clues and controversial discoveries that challenge our understanding of reality.

One such discovery emerged from the dusty surface of Mars, where a mysterious formation resembling a human face stared back at us from the Cydonia region. Initially dismissed as a trick of light and shadow, this "Face on Mars" ignited debates and inspired a dedicated group of researchers determined to uncover the truth. Among them was Richard Hoagland, a former NASA consultant and science advisor, who became a leading advocate for the idea that this formation—and others like it—could be evidence of an ancient extraterrestrial civilization.

Hoagland's pursuit of this possibility didn't stop at Mars. He turned his attention to our closest celestial neighbor, the Moon, where he claimed to find evidence of massive, artificial structures in NASA's photographs. These claims, if validated, would not only rewrite history but also raise profound questions about the transparency of governmental agencies tasked with exploring space.

In this chapter, we delve into the controversial world of UFOs and alleged extraterrestrial interventions. We explore the discoveries, the skeptics, the believers, and the underlying tensions that make this topic both fascinating and contentious. The urgency to unveil the truth isn't just about satisfying curiosity; it's about confronting the potential implications for humanity's future and our understanding of the universe.

The Face on Mars: A Tantalizing Glimpse into the Unknown

In 1976, NASA's Viking 1 orbiter was conducting a photographic survey of the Martian surface when it captured an image that would become one of the most debated photographs in the history of space exploration. In the Cydonia region of Mars, a formation resembling a human face appeared—a colossal structure seemingly gazing into space. To some, it was nothing more than a natural rock formation shaped by eons of erosion. To others, it was a deliberate construct, a message from an ancient civilization that once thrived on the Red Planet.

Richard Hoagland, a science writer and former NASA consultant, was among those captivated by the image. He and a group of like-minded researchers formed what became known as The Mars Mission, dedicating themselves to analyzing the Viking images with meticulous detail. Using advanced imaging techniques and computer analysis, they argued that the "Face on Mars" was symmetrical and bore features too precise to be the result of natural geological processes.

But the face wasn't the only anomaly. Nearby, other formations suggested the presence of a complex—pyramids, structures, and patterns that hinted at intelligent design. Hoagland proposed that these formations were part of a larger network of artifacts left behind by an advanced civilization, possibly providing clues about Mars' past and its connection to Earth.

The scientific community, however, was largely skeptical. Many dismissed the face as a classic example of pareidolia—the human tendency to perceive meaningful patterns, such as faces, in random or ambiguous visual data. Subsequent missions to Mars, including the Mars Global Surveyor, provided higher-resolution images that seemed to diminish the facial features, reinforcing the idea that it was a natural formation.

Yet, Hoagland and his supporters remained undeterred. They argued that NASA was selectively releasing images and that the agency had a vested interest in downplaying the significance of the Cydonia region. The debate highlighted a growing distrust among some members of the public toward governmental institutions and fueled speculation about hidden agendas.

Lost Opportunities: The Mars Observer Mission

The quest to uncover the mysteries of Mars suffered a significant setback in 1993 when NASA's Mars Observer spacecraft was lost just days before it was scheduled to enter Martian orbit. The mission, which had cost nearly a billion dollars, was designed to conduct a detailed photographic survey of the Martian surface, including the Cydonia region.

The loss of the Mars Observer was a blow not only to NASA but also to independent researchers like Hoagland, who hoped that new images might confirm their theories. Speculation about the cause of the loss ranged from technical malfunctions to more sinister explanations. Some suggested that the spacecraft was intentionally disabled to prevent the release of information that could validate the existence of extraterrestrial artifacts.

While such claims lacked concrete evidence, they underscored a persistent theme in the discourse around extraterrestrial life—the suspicion that governments and space agencies might be withholding information from the public. The Mars Observer's failure became another piece in the puzzle for those who believed that humanity's true history and place in the cosmos were being kept hidden.

Unveiling Secrets Closer to Home: Anomalies on the Moon

Not content with focusing solely on Mars, Richard Hoagland turned his investigative lens toward the Moon. Armed with thousands of NASA photographs from the Apollo missions and unmanned lunar orbiters, he began scrutinizing images for signs of artificial structures. What he claimed to find was nothing short of astounding.

Hoagland asserted that certain lunar regions contained remnants of colossal, glass-like structures—towers, domes, and geometric formations that defied conventional geological explanations. One of the most notable claims involved an alleged seven-mile-high tower in the Sinus Medii region, a central part of the Moon. This tower, according to Hoagland, appeared to be a partially preserved, crystalline structure, perhaps a remnant of an ancient lunar city.

The implications of such findings were profound. If the Moon harbored evidence of past extraterrestrial activity, it would suggest that Earth had been visited—or perhaps even influenced—by other intelligent beings. It would also raise questions about the history of the solar system and humanity's understanding of its origins.

Critics, however, were quick to challenge Hoagland's interpretations. They pointed out that the lunar environment is harsh, and the surface is heavily bombarded by micrometeorites and cosmic radiation, which can create unusual formations and optical illusions in photographs. Furthermore, image artifacts, film grain, and reflections could easily be misinterpreted as structures.

Despite the skepticism, Hoagland's claims gained a following, fueled by a desire among many to believe that we are not alone. His work also reignited debates about the transparency of NASA and whether the agency was fully disclosing all it knew about extraterrestrial phenomena.

The Brookings Report: A Policy of Silence?

One of the cornerstones of the argument that governmental agencies might suppress information about extraterrestrial life is the so-called Brookings Report. Commissioned by NASA in the early days of the space program, the 1960 report titled "Proposed Studies on the Implications of Peaceful Space Activities for Human Affairs" examined the potential societal impact of discovering extraterrestrial life.

The report discussed various scenarios, including the detection of radio signals from intelligent life and the discovery of artifacts on other planets. Notably, it suggested that such discoveries could have profound effects on society, potentially leading to social disintegration. The report recommended that, in the event of such discoveries, careful consideration should be given to whether and how to inform the public.

Hoagland and others have cited the Brookings Report as evidence that NASA—and by extension, the government—might have a policy of withholding information about extraterrestrial life to prevent societal upheaval. They argue that this policy could explain why certain data, such as the lunar anomalies Hoagland claims to have found, are not widely publicized or are actively suppressed.

It's important to note that the Brookings Report was speculative and advisory. It did not mandate any specific actions, nor is there evidence that its recommendations were adopted as official policy. Nevertheless, the report has become a focal point for those who believe in government secrecy surrounding extraterrestrial matters.

NASA and the Question of Transparency

The notion that NASA might be hiding evidence of extraterrestrial life is a serious allegation. NASA, as a publicly funded agency, operates under principles of openness and scientific integrity. The vast majority of its data, including images and research findings, are made publicly available.

However, in the realm of UFOs and extraterrestrial theories, NASA often finds itself at the center of controversy. The agency's explanations for various anomalies—be they on Mars, the Moon, or elsewhere—are sometimes met with skepticism by those who suspect a cover-up. The absence of definitive proof either way fuels ongoing debates.

For instance, when higher-resolution images of the Cydonia region were released, showing the "Face on Mars" to be a natural mesa, proponents of the artificial structure theory claimed that the images were manipulated or that NASA was focusing on specific angles to downplay the facial features.

Similarly, NASA's responses to claims of lunar structures have emphasized natural geological processes and the limitations of photographic technology from the era of the Apollo missions. Yet, for those convinced of a cover-up, these explanations are seen as evasive or incomplete.

The challenge lies in the extraordinary nature of the claims. As the saying goes, extraordinary claims require extraordinary evidence. While anomalies and unexplained phenomena certainly exist, interpreting them as definitive proof of extraterrestrial activity demands rigorous scrutiny.

Extraterrestrial Contact and the Human Psyche

The allure of discovering intelligent life beyond Earth taps into deep-seated human desires and fears. It's a theme that permeates our culture, from ancient myths to modern science fiction. Films like "Stargate," which explore the idea of extraterrestrial beings influencing human history, capture the imagination and reflect our collective curiosity.

Hoagland noted that the public's fascination with such stories indicates an "archetypal compulsion" to seek answers about our origins and place in the universe. This compulsion drives both scientific inquiry and speculative theories. It also creates a fertile ground for debates between skeptics and believers.

The popularity of extraterrestrial themes in media can both inform and distort public perception. On one hand, it raises awareness and stimulates interest in space exploration and the search for life. On the other hand, it can blur the lines between fiction and reality, making it challenging to separate evidence-based conclusions from imaginative speculation.

This dynamic plays out in the discussions surrounding UFOs, government disclosure, and alleged extraterrestrial interventions. The passionate beliefs on both sides often lead to polarized views, with little room for a middle ground.

SETI: Searching for Signals in the Silence

The Search for Extraterrestrial Intelligence (SETI) represents the scientific community's systematic efforts to detect signs of intelligent life beyond Earth. Using radio telescopes, SETI projects scan the skies for signals that could indicate the presence of technologically advanced civilizations.

While SETI operates with transparency and scientific rigor, it has faced criticism from various quarters. Hoagland, for instance, has dismissed SETI as a "complete, absolute farce," suggesting that it serves as a distraction rather than a genuine effort to find extraterrestrial intelligence. He argues that if evidence already exists—such as artifacts on Mars or the Moon—then SETI's approach is misguided.

Proponents of SETI counter that the search is a long-term endeavor that requires patience and persistence. The absence of detected signals so far doesn't invalidate the effort; rather, it highlights the vastness of space and the challenges inherent in making contact across cosmic distances.

The debate touches on fundamental questions about the best methods for seeking extraterrestrial life. Should we focus on listening for signals, searching for microbial life within our solar system, or interpreting anomalies in planetary geology? Each approach has its merits and limitations.

Crop Circles: Messages or Misinterpretations?

Among the more controversial phenomena linked to extraterrestrial theories are crop circles—complex patterns that appear mysteriously in fields, primarily in the United Kingdom but also in other parts of the world. Some believe that these formations are messages from extraterrestrial beings, encoded with advanced mathematical and scientific information.

Hoagland has suggested that crop circles could be part of an ongoing attempt by extraterrestrials to communicate with humanity. He points to the complexity and precision of certain formations as evidence that they are beyond human capability, or at least beyond the capabilities of hoaxers.

Skeptics argue that crop circles are the work of human artists and pranksters. Indeed, several individuals have come forward over the years claiming responsibility for creating specific crop circles, demonstrating the techniques used to produce them.

The crop circle debate illustrates the broader challenges in investigating unexplained phenomena. Without verifiable evidence, interpretations often rely on subjective assessments and the predispositions of those involved.

Conspiracy Theories and the Fog of Misinformation

In the landscape of UFOs and extraterrestrial intervention, conspiracy theories abound. Claims of government cover-ups, secret treaties with alien species, and clandestine organizations manipulating information are prevalent. Hoagland himself has speculated that disinformation campaigns might be in place to confuse the public and discredit legitimate evidence of extraterrestrial contact.

The proliferation of misinformation makes it difficult to discern truth from fabrication. In the age of the internet and social media, unverified claims can spread rapidly, gaining traction before they can be adequately scrutinized.

This environment can also be exploited by those seeking to manipulate public opinion or sow discord. The challenge for researchers and the public alike is to maintain a critical yet open-minded approach, seeking evidence and applying rigorous standards of proof.

The Call for Independent Exploration

Given the controversies and alleged secrecy surrounding governmental space agencies, some, like Hoagland, have advocated for privately funded missions to explore extraterrestrial anomalies. The idea is that independent exploration could bypass potential institutional roadblocks and bring transparency to the investigation.

Hoagland has proposed missions to the Moon to capture high-resolution images of the alleged structures, using modern technology to provide clear evidence one way or the other. The feasibility of such missions has increased with advancements in space technology and the emergence of private space companies.

However, mounting such missions requires significant financial resources and technical expertise. Moreover, even if successful, the interpretation of findings would still be subject to debate. Skeptics might question the authenticity of the data, and without peer-reviewed validation, conclusions might not gain widespread acceptance.

Nonetheless, the push for independent exploration underscores a broader desire for transparency and the democratization of space research. It reflects a belief that the quest to understand our universe should not be limited to governmental institutions.

The Urgency of Unveiling the Truth

At the heart of these discussions lies a profound urgency. If evidence of extraterrestrial life exists—especially intelligent life—it could have transformative implications for humanity. It could challenge our understanding of biology, technology, culture, and even spirituality.

The possibility that we are not alone raises questions about how we would interact with other intelligent beings, how we might learn from them, and how it could affect our society. Conversely, if such evidence is being withheld, it raises ethical concerns about who has the right to control such information.

The urgency also stems from a recognition that humanity faces significant challenges—environmental crises, technological risks, and social tensions. Some believe that understanding our place in a larger cosmic context could help us address these issues with greater wisdom.

In pursuing these questions, it's essential to balance open-minded inquiry with critical thinking. Extraordinary claims require thorough investigation and robust evidence. The quest to unveil the truth is not just about finding answers but also about refining our methods of inquiry and strengthening the integrity of our search.

The exploration of UFOs and potential extraterrestrial interventions is a journey that traverses the boundaries of science, philosophy, and human imagination. It challenges us to confront the unknown and to grapple with mysteries that may redefine our understanding of reality.

Whether we ultimately discover definitive evidence of extraterrestrial life or not, the pursuit itself enriches our collective endeavor to comprehend the universe. It pushes us to ask deeper questions, expand our horizons, and embrace the vast possibilities that lie beyond our current knowledge.

In the end, the search for extraterrestrial intelligence is also a search for ourselves—a quest to understand who we are, where we come from, and what our destiny might be in the grand arras of the cosmos.

Chapter 14: The Mystery of Atlantis and Lemuria

The depths of our oceans hold secrets that challenge the very foundations of our understanding of human history. Among these mysteries are the tales of Atlantis and Lemuria—legendary civilizations said to have vanished beneath the waves long before recorded history began. While mainstream archaeology often dismisses these stories as mere myths, recent underwater discoveries suggest that there may be more truth to these legends than previously thought.

In this chapter, we delve into the secret underwater structures discovered near Okinawa, Japan, and explore their potential connections to ancient, possibly pre-diluvian civilizations. We will examine the evidence, the controversies, and the implications of these findings on our perception of human history. The urgency of this investigation lies not only in unraveling the past but also in understanding the forces that could have wiped out entire civilizations—lessons that are increasingly relevant in our modern world.

Depiction of underwater structures near Okinawa

The Unexpected Discovery off Okinawa's Coast

In the spring of 1995, a recreational diver exploring the waters off the southern coast of Okinawa stumbled upon something that defied conventional understanding. While navigating through the clear blue depths, he encountered a massive stone structure, heavily encrusted with coral and marine life. The formation was not a natural outcropping or a simple reef; it appeared to be a colossal building, constructed from enormous stone blocks arranged in a way that suggested deliberate design.

The diver's photographs, shared with Japanese newspapers, ignited a firestorm of curiosity and controversy. Was this structure a remnant of a forgotten military installation from World War II, or was it something far older—evidence of an ancient civilization lost to the sea?

Expanding Discoveries and Growing Mysteries

The initial discovery prompted a flurry of activity among divers, archaeologists, and researchers. As teams began to systematically explore the area, they uncovered additional structures scattered across the ocean floor near Okinawa and its neighboring islands, including Yonaguni, Kerama, and Aguni. These findings were not isolated; they spanned a distance of over 300 miles, suggesting the remnants of a vast, interconnected complex.

The underwater structures varied in depth from twenty to over one hundred feet and exhibited remarkable architectural diversity. Among the discoveries were:

- **Paved streets and crossroads**: Indicating sophisticated urban planning.
- **Massive stone staircases**: Led to expansive plazas that may have served as public gathering spaces or ceremonial sites.
- **Altar-like formations and towering pylons**: Suggesting religious or ritualistic functions.
- **An enormous arch or gateway**: Constructed from precisely fitted megalithic blocks, reminiscent of ancient masonry techniques found in other parts of the world.

The scale and complexity of these structures challenged the conventional timeline of human civilization in the region. The possibility that they could be over 10,000 years old—dating back to a time when sea levels were significantly lower—raised profound questions about our understanding of ancient history.

The Debate: Natural Formations or Human Constructions?

From the outset, the scientific community was divided over the origins of the underwater structures. Skeptics argued that the formations were natural geological features, sculpted by tectonic activity and erosion. Proponents of the man-made hypothesis pointed to the precise angles, straight edges, and geometric patterns that seemed unlikely to occur through natural processes alone.

Geological Perspectives

Geologists noted that the area around Okinawa is tectonically active, with frequent earthquakes and shifts in the Earth's crust. They suggested that natural fracturing and erosion could produce formations that mimic human architecture. The layering of sedimentary rock and the presence of jointing patterns could, over millennia, result in structures with sharp angles and flat surfaces.

Archaeological and Anthropological Arguments

Archaeologists and anthropologists who supported the man-made theory highlighted several key points:

- **Precision of Construction**: The structures featured right angles, flat surfaces, and interlocking blocks that suggested deliberate shaping and assembly.
- **Cultural Parallels**: Similarities to ancient constructions found in other parts of the world, such as the pyramids of Central and South America, and the megalithic sites in Polynesia and Micronesia.
- **Absence of Known Natural Processes**: The specific features of the structures did not align neatly with any known natural geological processes, making the natural formation hypothesis less convincing.

Global Connections: Parallels with Other Ancient Sites

One of the most compelling aspects of the Okinawa structures is their resemblance to ancient sites across the globe. This raises the possibility of a lost, advanced civilization that could have been the progenitor of cultures in both the Eastern and Western hemispheres.

Similarities with South American Sites

The architecture of the underwater structures bears a striking resemblance to pre-Incan constructions in Peru. For instance, the massive stepped platforms and terraces are reminiscent of the pyramids at Pachacamac and the Moche pyramids near Trujillo. These sites, built thousands of years ago, feature large stone blocks assembled with remarkable precision.

Connections to Polynesian Megaliths

The Polynesian islands, scattered across the Pacific Ocean, are home to numerous megalithic structures that share characteristics with the Okinawa discoveries. The **heiau** of Hawaii, ancient temples constructed from stone, feature long ramparts leading to elevated platforms, much like the underwater formations near Okinawa.

Additionally, the legends of the **Menehune**, a race of master builders in Hawaiian mythology, parallel stories of ancient, advanced civilizations that predate known history.

The Enigmatic Torii Gates of Japan

In Japan, the **torii** gate is a traditional structure that marks the entrance to a sacred space. These gates, often made of wood or stone, symbolize the transition from the mundane to the spiritual. The underwater gateway discovered near Okinawa mirrors this cultural motif, suggesting a ceremonial or religious significance.

The presence of similar gate structures in distant cultures, such as the **Ha'amonga 'a Maui** in Tonga and the ceremonial gates of Tiahuanaco in Bolivia, hints at a shared architectural or symbolic tradition that spans continents.

Legends and Linguistic Clues: The Tales of Mu and Lemuria

The legends of lost continents like Mu and Lemuria have been part of global mythology for centuries. These stories often describe advanced civilizations that perished due to cataclysmic events, leaving behind scattered survivors and submerged ruins.

The Legend of Mu

In various Pacific Island cultures, Mu is referred to as a motherland or ancestral homeland that was lost beneath the sea. The Hawaiian **Kumulipo**, an ancient creation chant, speaks of a great flood that devastated the world, echoing flood myths found in cultures worldwide.

The term **mu** in Japanese and Korean means "that which does not exist" or "no longer exists," possibly referencing a land that vanished. Moreover, the presence of words like **moai**—used both in Okinawa to describe ancestral burial vaults and on Easter Island to denote the famous statues—suggests linguistic connections across vast distances.

The Enigma of Lemuria

Lemuria, another hypothesized lost continent, was once believed by some scientists to have connected Africa, India, and Southeast Asia, explaining the distribution of certain species like lemurs. Although modern geology has debunked the existence of such a continent, the myth persists, intertwined with legends of ancient civilizations.

In Roman mythology, the **Lemuria** was a festival to exorcise malevolent spirits, possibly derived from older traditions linked to a sunken landmass.

Scientific Expeditions and Controversies

The discoveries near Okinawa attracted the attention of prominent researchers, including geologist Dr. Robert M. Schoch, known for his work on the Sphinx water erosion hypothesis, and authors like John Anthony West and Graham Hancock, who explore alternative histories of human civilization.

The 1997 Yonaguni Expedition

In 1997, Schoch, West, and Hancock conducted dives to investigate the Yonaguni Monument, one of the most prominent underwater structures. Their findings were mixed:

- **Schoch's Skepticism**: Dr. Schoch suggested that while the formations were unusual, they could be natural, enhanced by human modification.
- **West's Cautious Approach**: John Anthony West emphasized the need for further research before drawing definitive conclusions.
- **Hancock's Openness**: Graham Hancock remained open to the possibility of a lost civilization, advocating for more extensive exploration.

Their expedition highlighted the challenges in studying underwater sites: limited accessibility, preservation issues, and the difficulty in distinguishing natural formations from human-made structures.

Critiques and Counterarguments

Skeptics argue that the lack of artifacts—such as tools, pottery, or human remains—weakens the case for a lost civilization. They emphasize the importance of rigorous scientific methodology and caution against drawing sensational conclusions without substantial evidence.

Proponents counter that the strong ocean currents and the passage of millennia could have swept away or buried such artifacts. They also point to similar underwater discoveries elsewhere, such as the submerged city of Dwarka in India, as evidence that ancient civilizations may indeed lie beneath the seas.

The Implications of Rising Sea Levels and Catastrophic Events

Understanding the potential antiquity of the underwater structures requires examining the geological history of sea levels and tectonic activity.

Sea Level Changes

At the end of the last Ice Age, around 12,000 years ago, melting glaciers caused global sea levels to rise by over 100 meters. Vast tracts of coastal land were inundated, potentially submerging settlements and wiping out evidence of early civilizations.

If the Okinawa structures date back to this period, they could represent a civilization that thrived before the dramatic sea level rise—a civilization that mainstream archaeology has yet to acknowledge.

Tectonic Activity and Land Subsidence

Japan sits atop multiple tectonic plates, making it one of the most seismically active regions on Earth. Earthquakes and volcanic activity can lead to sudden land subsidence or uplift, dramatically altering the landscape.

It's possible that the underwater structures sank gradually due to tectonic shifts or were submerged suddenly due to catastrophic events.

Revisiting Ancient Myths with a Critical Eye

The intersection of legend and archaeology invites us to reconsider ancient myths as potential repositories of historical truth.

Flood Myths as Historical Records

Nearly every culture has a flood myth, from the biblical story of Noah's Ark to the Mesopotamian Epic of Gilgamesh. These stories may reflect collective memories of real events—massive floods caused by melting ice caps or tsunamis triggered by asteroid impacts or volcanic eruptions.

Reevaluating these myths with modern scientific understanding could provide insights into prehistoric events that shaped human history.

The Case for a Lost Advanced Civilization

While the notion of a highly advanced civilization existing tens of thousands of years ago remains controversial, discoveries like Göbekli Tepe in Turkey—a sophisticated temple complex dated to around 12,000 years ago—challenge the conventional timeline of societal development.

If such a civilization did exist, its remnants could lie beneath the oceans, waiting to be discovered. The underwater structures near Okinawa might be a piece of this puzzle.

The Urgent Need for Further Exploration

The potential significance of the Okinawa underwater structures cannot be overstated. They represent a unique opportunity to explore the depths of human history and possibly rewrite our understanding of ancient civilizations.

Technological Advances in Underwater Archaeology

Modern technology offers new tools for exploration:

- **Advanced Diving Equipment**: Allows for longer and deeper dives.
- **Remote Operated Vehicles (ROVs)**: Can access depths and areas too dangerous for divers.

- **Sonar Mapping and 3D Imaging**: Provide detailed views of underwater sites without physical disturbance.
- **Submersibles**: Manned and unmanned submersibles enable direct observation and sampling.

Utilizing these technologies could help researchers map the full extent of the structures, identify any artifacts, and conduct precise dating.

International Collaboration and Funding

Given the scope and potential impact of the research, international collaboration is essential. Pooling resources and expertise can accelerate discoveries and ensure that investigations meet the highest scientific standards.

Securing funding remains a challenge, as underwater archaeology is expensive and time-consuming. However, the possible rewards—in terms of knowledge and cultural heritage—justify the investment.

Confronting the Resistance of Mainstream Academia

One of the significant obstacles to advancing research on Okinawa structures and similar sites is the reluctance of mainstream academia to engage with unconventional hypotheses. The adherence to established timelines and narratives can stifle the exploration of alternative possibilities.

The Risk of Intellectual Complacency

Dismissing new evidence because it doesn't fit existing models hampers scientific progress. True scholarship requires openness to new data and the willingness to revise theories in light of new findings.

Encouraging Academic Debate

Constructive debate and peer review are cornerstones of the scientific method. By fostering respectful dialogue between skeptics and proponents, the academic community can collectively work towards uncovering the truth.

The mystery of the underwater structures near Okinawa remains unsolved. Whether they are natural formations, human-made constructions, or a combination of both, their existence challenges us to look deeper—both literally and figuratively.

The legends of Atlantis and Lemuria, long relegated to the realm of myth, may hold kernels of historical reality. As we stand at the intersection of myth, archaeology, and geology, we have the opportunity—and perhaps the responsibility—to pursue these mysteries with vigor and open-mindedness.

The urgency of this pursuit lies not only in satisfying our curiosity but in understanding the fragility of civilizations. If advanced societies did exist and were wiped out by natural catastrophes, their stories serve as cautionary tales for our own time.

In the depths of the ocean, the echoes of ancient worlds await discovery. It is up to us to listen, to explore, and to learn from the past before the opportunity slips away.

Chapter 15: The Secrets of Our Planets

For centuries, the notion of a prehistoric civilization destroyed by a cataclysmic flood has captivated the imagination of scholars and laypeople alike. Plato's account of Atlantis is perhaps the most famous of these stories, hinting at a lost world swallowed by the sea. Yet, despite the plethora of myths and legends from cultures worldwide that speak of a great deluge, mainstream science has largely dismissed these accounts as mere folklore.

In the 19th century, as evidence of massive water erosion and deposits became too significant to ignore, the scientific establishment faced a crossroads. They could acknowledge the possibility of a global flood—an event that aligned uncomfortably with biblical narratives—or they could devise an alternative explanation that fits within their secular worldview. They chose the latter, and thus the Ice Age was born.

The Ice Age theory posits that immense glaciers once covered vast portions of the Earth, slowly shaping the landscape over millennia. This idea provided a convenient explanation for the geological features that suggested catastrophic flooding. It allowed scientists to sidestep the implications of a global flood and maintain a uniformitarian view of Earth's history—the belief that the same gradual processes we observe today have always been at work.

However, this theory was not without its problems. Glaciers, as we understand them, move due to gravity, flowing from higher elevations to lower ones. They cannot explain the presence of massive boulders—erratics—found in places where no glacier could have transported them. Nor do they account for the mixed remains of tropical and arctic fauna found together in the same sediment layers, suggesting a sudden and violent upheaval rather than a slow, glacial process.

The insistence on the Ice Age as the sole explanation for these phenomena reveals a deeper issue within the scientific community: a reluctance to consider alternative theories that challenge entrenched paradigms. This resistance is not merely about differing interpretations of data; it reflects a systemic suppression of ideas that threaten the established order.

The Suppression of Alternative Histories

Throughout history, there have been numerous accounts and pieces of evidence pointing toward the existence of advanced prehistoric civilizations. Megalithic structures found across the globe—pyramids, stone circles, and other monumental constructions—hint at a level of technological and societal development that seems incongruent with the conventional timeline of human history.

Researchers like Graham Hancock and Robert M. Schoch have argued that these structures are remnants of a lost civilization that was destroyed by catastrophic floods. They point to geological and linguistic evidence, as well as ancient myths and legends, to support their claims. Yet, their work has often been met with skepticism or outright hostility from the academic establishment.

This pattern of suppression is not new. In the late 19th and early 20th centuries, evidence of advanced ancient cultures in North America was systematically destroyed or ignored. Major John Wesley Powell, a prominent figure in American science, led efforts to dismiss or eliminate findings that suggested pre-Columbian transoceanic contact or the existence of non-native civilizations. His actions were part of a broader movement to maintain the narrative of isolated cultural development and to prevent any challenges to the prevailing historical models.

The reluctance to accept alternative histories is rooted in a fear of the implications such acceptance would have. Acknowledging a prehistoric advanced civilization—and its destruction by a global flood—would require a reevaluation of fundamental scientific and historical assumptions. It would also blur the lines between myth and history, forcing scholars to reconsider the validity of ancient narratives that have long been dismissed as mere stories.

Immanuel Velikovsky and the Martyrdom of a Visionary

Perhaps no figure embodies the struggle against scientific orthodoxy more than Immanuel Velikovsky. A man of immense intellect and diverse expertise, Velikovsky dared to challenge the foundational principles of astronomy, geology, and history. His work serves as a case study of how revolutionary ideas are often met with vehement opposition from the very institutions that claim to champion open inquiry.

Velikovsky's journey began with a simple yet profound question: Could the catastrophes described in ancient texts, such as the plagues of Egypt in the Bible, have a basis in real astronomical events? His research led him to propose that planetary bodies, particularly Venus and Mars, had played a direct role in Earth's history through close encounters and electromagnetic interactions.

In his groundbreaking book, *Worlds in Collision*, Velikovsky argued that Venus was ejected as a comet from Jupiter and had passed near Earth within human history, causing massive disruptions that were recorded in the myths and legends of cultures worldwide. He suggested that electromagnetic forces, not just gravity, played a significant role in planetary motions—an idea that was radical for its time.

The response from the scientific community was swift and brutal. Velikovsky faced a concerted campaign to discredit his work and destroy his reputation. Prominent scientists, without even reading his book, pressured publishers to drop him, orchestrated smear campaigns, and ostracized him from academic circles. The intensity of the backlash was disproportionate, revealing an underlying fear of the implications of his theories.

Yet, over time, many of Velikovsky's predictions were validated. The discovery of radio emissions from Jupiter, the high temperatures of Venus, and evidence of electromagnetic phenomena in space all aligned with his assertions. Despite this, the scientific establishment has been reluctant to acknowledge his contributions, preferring to let his name fade into obscurity.

Catastrophism vs. Uniformitarianism: A Battle for Earth's History

At the heart of the conflict between Velikovsky and his detractors lies a fundamental disagreement over the nature of Earth's history. Uniformitarianism, the dominant paradigm, holds that geological and astronomical processes have always occurred gradually and consistently over vast periods. Catastrophism, on the other hand, acknowledges that sudden, violent events have played a significant role in shaping the planet.

The uniformitarian view provides a sense of comfort and stability, suggesting that the world operates according to predictable laws and that dramatic changes are rare exceptions. Catastrophism introduces an element of unpredictability and chaos, implying that the Earth—and humanity—are vulnerable to forces beyond our control.

The evidence for catastrophism is compelling. Geological formations that defy gradual explanations, mass extinction events, and the rich tapestry of global myths recounting cosmic upheavals all point toward a history punctuated by sudden, catastrophic occurrences.

Moreover, recent scientific advancements have begun to erode the strict uniformitarian perspective. The recognition of asteroid impacts as contributors to mass extinctions, the observation of extreme space weather events, and the acknowledgment of rapid climate shifts all support a more nuanced understanding that incorporates both gradual and catastrophic processes.

Yet, despite this growing evidence, the reluctance to fully embrace catastrophism persists. This resistance stems not from a lack of data but from a deep-seated attachment to existing frameworks. Admitting that our planet's history includes periods of immense disruption challenges not only scientific models but also our collective sense of security.

The Role of Ancient Myths and Legends

One of the most significant barriers to accepting alternative historical narratives is the dismissal of ancient myths and legends as mere fiction. However, these stories often contain kernels of truth, preserving the memories of real events that occurred in the distant past.

Velikovsky recognized that cultures worldwide shared remarkably similar tales of cosmic battles, floods, and celestial dragons. He saw these as accounts of actual astronomical events witnessed by our ancestors. By interpreting these myths through a scientific lens, he sought to uncover the hidden history of planetary interactions that had profound impacts on Earth.

This approach requires a willingness to bridge disciplines, combining mythology, astronomy, geology, and psychology. It challenges the compartmentalization of knowledge that is prevalent in academia, where specialists often remain isolated within their fields.

The work of scholars like David Talbott and Wallace Thornhill continues this interdisciplinary exploration. They argue that the celestial events described in ancient narratives reflect a time when planets moved close to Earth, leading to dramatic electrical interactions observable in the sky. These encounters left an indelible mark on human consciousness, influencing religions, symbols, and cultural practices.

By reevaluating myths as historical records, we open the door to a deeper understanding of our past. We acknowledge that our ancestors may have witnessed phenomena that we have not experienced and that their accounts, though couched in symbolic language, hold valuable insights into Earth's history.

The Electric Universe: Rethinking Planetary Science

One of the most intriguing developments arising from this line of inquiry is the concept of the Electric Universe. Proponents like Thornhill suggest that electromagnetic forces play a far more significant role in the cosmos than mainstream science recognizes.

Traditional astronomy emphasizes gravity as the primary force governing celestial bodies. However, the behavior of plasma—the most abundant form of visible matter in the universe—indicates that electric and magnetic fields are also crucial. Plasma conducts electricity and can carry electrical currents over vast distances, forming structures like Birkeland currents observed in space.

The Electric Universe theory proposes that stars, including our Sun, are not solely powered by nuclear fusion at their cores but also by external electric currents flowing through the galaxy. This perspective offers alternative explanations for various astronomical phenomena, such as the high temperatures of the solar corona, the behavior of comets, and the peculiarities of planetary magnetospheres.

Applying this framework to planetary science, we can reinterpret the geological features observed on planets and moons. For example, the sinuous rilles on the Moon and Mars, traditionally explained as collapsed lava tubes or riverbeds, may instead be the result of electrical arcing—massive cosmic lightning bolts carving the surface.

If such events occurred within human history, as suggested by ancient accounts, they would have been awe-inspiring and terrifying, leaving a lasting legacy in human culture.

The Psychological Impact of Suppressed History

The suppression of alternative historical narratives has consequences beyond academic discourse. It affects our collective psyche, shaping how we perceive ourselves and our place in the universe.

Velikovsky posited that humanity suffers from a form of collective amnesia, a psychological repression of traumatic events from our distant past. The denial of these memories manifests in various ways, including persistent myths, ritualistic behaviors, and even patterns of violence.

By refusing to acknowledge the possibility of catastrophic events that dramatically altered human history, we limit our understanding of human behavior and societal development. We also impede our ability to prepare for or mitigate future catastrophes.

Furthermore, the suppression of alternative ideas fosters a culture of intellectual conformity. It discourages critical thinking and stifles innovation. When challenging the status quo is met with hostility rather than open debate, progress becomes hindered by dogma.

The Need for Open Inquiry and Interdisciplinary Research

The case of Velikovsky and the ongoing debates about Earth's history highlight the importance of open inquiry and the integration of knowledge across disciplines. No single field holds all the answers, and complex questions often require holistic approaches.

Science advances through the testing of hypotheses and the willingness to consider new evidence, even when it contradicts established theories. Suppressing ideas because they challenge prevailing paradigms undermines the very foundation of scientific endeavor.

Interdisciplinary research fosters creativity and can lead to breakthroughs that isolated disciplines might miss. By combining insights from astronomy, geology, mythology, psychology, and other fields, we can develop more comprehensive models of Earth's history and the dynamics of our solar system.

Embracing the Unknown

The secrets of our planets are not just about the physical characteristics of celestial bodies but about understanding the forces that have shaped our world and humanity's journey within it. Acknowledging that there is much we do not know—and that some of what we think we know may be incorrect—is a vital step toward deeper knowledge.

Embracing alternative theories does not mean accepting them uncritically. It means being open to investigation, allowing evidence to guide conclusions rather than letting conclusions dictate what evidence is permissible.

In acknowledging the efforts of those like Immanuel Velikovsky, who dared to challenge the orthodoxies of their time, we honor the spirit of inquiry that drives human progress. We recognize that the pursuit of truth often requires courage in the face of opposition.

Chapter 16: The Future of Forbidden Paleoliths History

Imagine a world where the chronicles of human history are far more ancient than we've ever been told. A world where the footprints of our ancestors stretch back not mere thousands, but millions of years. For too long, the gatekeepers of conventional science have dismissed, ignored, or outright suppressed evidence that challenges the established timeline of human evolution. But the truth, buried beneath layers of sediment and skepticism, refuses to stay hidden.

In this chapter, we embark on a journey to uncover the future of forbidden paleolithic history—a future that demands we rewrite the annals of our past. We'll delve into controversial discoveries, meet the maverick scientists who dared to defy orthodoxy and confront the uncomfortable questions that arise when long-held beliefs are challenged by undeniable evidence.

The Conundrum of Eoliths and Paleoliths

Before diving into the contentious discoveries, it's crucial to understand the difference between eoliths and paleoliths—terms that categorize the earliest known stone tools. Eoliths are naturally broken stones that show minimal signs of human modification. They might exhibit slight wear or minor retouching but are largely unaltered by deliberate human activity. Paleoliths, on the other hand, are stones that have been intentionally flaked from cores and extensively modified to serve specific purposes. They represent a significant technological advancement over eoliths, indicating a higher level of cognitive function and manual dexterity among their makers.

The debate surrounding these artifacts centers on whether certain stone tools are the result of human craftsmanship or natural geological processes. This distinction is pivotal because it influences our understanding of when intelligent hominids first appeared on Earth.

Carlos Ribeiro's Pioneering Discoveries in Portugal

In the mid-19th century, Carlos Ribeiro, a respected geologist appointed to head the Geological Survey of Portugal, made groundbreaking discoveries that shook the foundations of paleoanthropology. While investigating the Tertiary formations in the Tagus River basin near Lisbon, Ribeiro unearthed flint tools embedded in Miocene strata—geological layers dating back approximately 5 to 23 million years.

Initially hesitant due to prevailing scientific dogmas that confined human existence to the Quaternary period (the last 2.6 million years), Ribeiro cautiously classified these findings as Quaternary. However, upon further examination and influenced by the work of contemporaries like Edouard de Verneuil and Abbé Louis Bourgeois—who reported similar findings in France—Ribeiro boldly asserted that these implements were indeed from the Tertiary period.

At various international congresses, Ribeiro presented his collection of flint tools, which exhibited clear signs of human workmanship. Features such as bulbs of percussion and striking platforms indicated deliberate crafting. Despite some skepticism, prominent scientists like Gabriel de Mortillet and Emile Cartailhac supported Ribeiro's claims after personally examining the artifacts.

The implications were staggering: if humans or their ancestors were crafting tools during the Miocene, our timeline of human evolution would need drastic revision. Yet, despite the compelling evidence, Ribeiro's discoveries were gradually dismissed and forgotten, overshadowed by the rigid adherence to established evolutionary models.

The Thenay Implements: Bourgeois's Battle for Recognition

Around the same time, the Abbé Louis Bourgeois discovered flint tools in the Early Miocene formations at Thenay, France. These artifacts bore striking similarities to known Quaternary implements, featuring retouching, symmetrical chipping, and usage wear consistent with human-made tools.

Bourgeois faced intense scrutiny and skepticism from the scientific community. Critics questioned the stratigraphic context of the finds, suggesting that the tools might have slipped into older layers through natural processes like fissures. Undeterred, Bourgeois conducted meticulous excavations, demonstrating that the tools were indeed embedded within undisturbed Miocene deposits.

A commission formed at the 1872 International Congress of Prehistoric Anthropology and Archeology ultimately supported Bourgeois, with a majority recognizing the artifacts as products of human craftsmanship. Despite this validation, the broader scientific community remained resistant, primarily because accepting such ancient human activity conflicted with the prevailing theories of human evolution.

Aurillac's Puzzling Artifacts: The Work of Charles Tardy and J. B. Rames

In the late 19th century, additional evidence emerged from Aurillac in southern France. Charles Tardy discovered a flint knife within Late Miocene conglomerate formations. While initial skepticism arose regarding the artifact's context, further excavations by J. B. Rames yielded more implements from the same geological period.

These tools included celts, scrapers, arrowheads, and flakes, all displaying intentional chipping and use-wear patterns indicative of human manufacture. Prominent anthropologists like Armand de Quatrefages and S. Laing acknowledged the significance of these finds, noting the presence of parallel flake scars and other hallmarks of deliberate tool production.

Max Verworn, a German scientist initially skeptical of such claims, conducted his investigations at Aurillac. After rigorous analysis, he concluded that the artifacts were indeed crafted by intelligent beings during the Late Miocene. Verworn's findings suggested the existence of a culture with a level of technological development previously unimagined for that era.

Rutot's Oligocene Artifacts in Belgium

Alphonse Rutot, conservator at the Royal Museum of Natural History in Brussels, made a series of remarkable discoveries in the early 20th century. In sandpits near Boncelles, he unearthed stone tools from Oligocene deposits—dating between 25 to 38 million years ago. The array of implements included choppers, knives, scrapers, borers, and throwing stones, all displaying clear signs of intentional modification.

Rutot's findings were met with both intrigue and disbelief. The notion that intelligent beings capable of crafting such tools existed during the Oligocene was too radical for many to accept. Yet, the artifacts bore undeniable evidence of human-like workmanship.

Freudenberg's Controversial Footprints and Tools Near Antwerp

In 1918, Wilhelm Freudenberg, a geologist working near Antwerp, Belgium, discovered flint objects, cut bones, shells, and even partial footprints in Scaldisian marine deposits (4 to 7 million years old). The footprints exhibited patterns of ridges and pores akin to human feet, distinct from those of apes.

Freudenberg suggested that a small hominid, possibly a precursor to modern humans, was responsible for these artifacts. However, this idea conflicted with established timelines that placed such beings in much more recent epochs. Consequently, his findings were largely dismissed or ignored by the mainstream scientific community.

Suppression and Dismissal: The Fate of Anomalous Discoveries

The recurring theme across these accounts is the systematic suppression, dismissal, or neglect of evidence that challenges established narratives of human history. When confronted with artifacts or fossils that suggest a much earlier human presence, the scientific community has often responded with skepticism rooted not in empirical analysis but in adherence to prevailing theories.

For instance, the lack of acknowledgment of Ribeiro's work in modern textbooks and academic discourse exemplifies how inconvenient evidence can be effectively erased from collective knowledge. Similarly, the reluctance to accept Bourgeois's Thenay implements, despite rigorous validation, highlights a tendency to prioritize theoretical consistency over empirical anomalies.

The Impact of Preconceived Notions on Scientific Inquiry

The resistance to these discoveries underscores a broader issue in scientific inquiry: the influence of preconceived notions and theoretical frameworks on the interpretation of evidence. When new data contradicts established theories, there is a tendency to question the data rather than the theory.

This approach hampers the advancement of knowledge by creating an environment where alternative hypotheses are not given fair consideration. It fosters a culture where researchers may fear professional repercussions for presenting findings that challenge the status quo, leading to self-censorship and the potential loss of valuable insights.

The Call for Reexamination and Open Discourse

The future of forbidden paleoliths history hinges on the willingness of the scientific community to reexamine these anomalous findings with an open mind. It requires acknowledging that our current understanding of human history may be incomplete or flawed. By revisiting these discoveries with modern analytical techniques and a commitment to unbiased investigation, we may uncover new dimensions of our past.

Advancements in dating methods, such as improved radiometric techniques, could provide more accurate assessments of the age of these artifacts. Additionally, interdisciplinary collaboration between archaeologists, geologists, anthropologists, and other specialists can yield a more holistic understanding of the context in which these tools were made and used.

Embracing a Multilinear Perspective of Human Evolution

One possible implication of these suppressed discoveries is that human evolution may not be a linear progression but a multilinear one, with multiple hominid species coexisting and exhibiting varying levels of technological and cognitive development. This perspective allows for the possibility that advanced tool-making capabilities emerged earlier and independently in different regions.

Such a model aligns with recent findings that suggest interbreeding between Homo sapiens, Neanderthals, and Denisovans. It opens the door to reevaluating the uniqueness of modern humans and understanding the contributions of other hominids to the development of technology and culture.

The Role of Technology in Unveiling the Past

Modern technology offers unprecedented opportunities to revisit these ancient sites and artifacts. Techniques like ground-penetrating radar, remote sensing, and high-precision dating can provide new insights without the need for invasive excavation. Micro-wear analysis and residue studies can reveal how tools were used, shedding light on the behaviors and capabilities of their makers.

Moreover, digital platforms and open-access databases enable the sharing of information across the global scientific community, fostering collaboration and cross-validation. By making data more accessible, we can encourage diverse perspectives and reduce the gatekeeping that has historically hindered the acceptance of controversial findings.

Confronting the Institutional Barriers to New Knowledge

For progress to occur, institutional barriers that impede the acceptance of paradigm-challenging evidence must be addressed. This involves:

1. **Reforming Peer Review Processes**: Ensuring that peer review is conducted fairly and without bias, allowing for the publication of rigorously researched findings regardless of their conformity to existing theories.
2. **Encouraging Academic Freedom**: Protecting researchers who pursue unconventional lines of inquiry from professional retaliation, including loss of funding or employment.
3. **Promoting Interdisciplinary Dialogue**: Facilitating communication between different fields to integrate various methodologies and perspectives in the analysis of evidence.
4. **Educating the Next Generation**: Incorporating discussions of these controversial findings into academic curricula to inspire critical thinking and openness to new ideas among students.

At the heart of this issue lies an ethical imperative: the pursuit of truth must supersede the comfort of consensus. Science advances through the challenging of assumptions and the rigorous testing of new hypotheses. Suppressing evidence not only hinders our understanding but also undermines the integrity of scientific endeavor.

By confronting these forbidden chapters of paleolithic history, we honor the spirit of inquiry that has driven human progress. We acknowledge that our ancestors may have been more complex and capable than previously believed, and we embrace the richness of a history that is still being written.

The future of forbidden paleoliths history is not just about reevaluating the past; it's about reshaping the methodologies and attitudes with which we approach the study of human origins. It calls for a paradigm shift that values evidence over entrenched theories, fosters open-mindedness, and prioritizes the collaborative pursuit of knowledge.

Chapter 17: Unveiling India's Hidden Legacy—The Indian Mystery

For centuries, scholars have grappled with the profound depths of India's past, often attempting to fit it within the confines of Western timelines and narratives. Yet, India's true history might be far older, more complex, and more astonishing than we have been led to believe.

In this chapter, we embark on a journey to unravel the Indian Mystery—a tale of lost continents, ancient advanced civilizations, and knowledge systems that predate recorded history. We will confront the biases that have suppressed this narrative and explore the evidence that suggests India was once the heart of a sophisticated and expansive civilization.

The Western Gaze: Misinterpretation and Suppression

For centuries, Western scholars have approached India's history through a lens tinted by ethnocentrism and a sense of intellectual superiority. The colonial era, in particular, saw European academics attempting to decode India's past while often dismissing or downplaying its rich traditions and ancient wisdom. This approach not only distorted the true nature of Indian civilization but also led to the suppression of knowledge that did not align with Western narratives.

The Imposition of Western Timelines

Western academia has long been obsessed with categorizing history into neat, linear timelines that often begin with Western civilizations as the pinnacle of human achievement. When faced with India's vast and intricate history, these scholars attempted to fit it into their preconceived frameworks. Ancient Indian texts that spoke of humanity's origins, lost continents, and advanced prehistoric civilizations were often labeled as myths or allegories, unworthy of serious consideration.

This dismissal wasn't merely a scholarly oversight; it was a deliberate act rooted in the desire to maintain a Eurocentric view of history. By undermining the credibility of ancient Indian traditions, Western scholars could assert the dominance of their narratives and suppress any evidence that challenged the established order.

The Knowledge Filter in Action

This systematic suppression of information is part of what some researchers refer to as the "knowledge filter." It's a phenomenon where data that doesn't fit accepted theories is ignored, ridiculed, or actively suppressed. In the context of India's history, the knowledge filter has been particularly effective. It has kept groundbreaking discoveries out of mainstream discourse and maintained the illusion that Western civilization is the cradle of all significant human development.

Lost Continents and Ancient Civilizations

One of the most intriguing aspects of the Indian Mystery is the concept of lost continents, particularly Lemuria—or Kumari Kandam, as referred to in Tamil traditions. The notion of a submerged landmass in the Indian Ocean challenges conventional geography and suggests that ancient civilizations may have thrived in regions now beneath the sea.

Lemuria: A Continent Forgotten

In the mid-19th century, geologists discovered striking similarities between fossils and sedimentary strata in India, South Africa, Australia, and South America. These findings led to the hypothesis that a massive landmass once connected these regions—a continent they named Lemuria. British biologist Philip

L. Sclater coined the term after studying the distribution of lemurs in Madagascar and India.

Lemuria became a topic of fascination, with various scholars and mystics delving into its possible history. Madame Helena Blavatsky, founder of the Theosophical Society, wrote extensively about Lemuria, suggesting it was home to an advanced civilization that predated recorded history. Later, Colonel James Churchward claimed to have discovered ancient tablets in India describing Mu, another name for this lost continent.

However, the advent of the theory of continental drift and plate tectonics in the 20th century led mainstream science to dismiss the existence of Lemuria. The slow movement of continents over millions of years seemed to leave little room for the sudden disappearance of a landmass within human history. Yet, this dismissal may have been premature.

Kumari Kandam: The Tamil Connection

In the ancient texts of southern India, particularly within Tamil literature, there are numerous references to a vast land known as Kumari Kandam. According to these texts, Kumari Kandam was a sprawling continent that connected present-day India to Madagascar and Australia. This land was said to have been ruled by the Pandiyan kings and was the cradle of the Tamil civilization.

The **Silappadhikaram**, one of the five great epics of Tamil literature, mentions Kumari Nadu (another name for Kumari Kandam) extensively. It describes a land rich in culture, with flourishing cities, rivers, and mountains teeming with life. The texts speak of a catastrophic deluge that submerged this continent, forcing its inhabitants to migrate to other parts of India and beyond.

These accounts are not isolated. Similar legends of sunken lands and ancient floods are found in the traditions of Sri Lanka, the Andaman Islands, and even among the indigenous peoples of the

Mergui Archipelago off the coast of Burma. Could these stories be remnants of collective memories of actual events?

Ancient Texts and Advanced Knowledge

India's ancient scriptures are replete with references to advanced technologies, sophisticated knowledge systems, and events that defy conventional historical timelines. The **Mahabharata** and the **Ramayana**, epic poems dated by some scholars to as early as the fifth millennium BCE, contain passages that have puzzled historians and scientists alike.

Vimana: The Ancient Flying Machines

One of the most fascinating aspects of these epics is the detailed descriptions of **vimanas**—mythical flying machines used by gods and heroes. These texts describe various types of vimanas, their construction, capabilities, and even the materials used to build them. For instance, the **Vaimanika Shastra**, a Sanskrit text discovered in the early 20th century, provides intricate details on aeronautics, suggesting knowledge of aviation long before the modern era.

These accounts challenge our understanding of ancient technology. Were these mere flights of fancy, or did they reflect a lost knowledge of advanced engineering? The specificity of the descriptions suggests the latter. Moreover, similar myths of flying machines are found in other ancient cultures, hinting at a shared heritage of forgotten technologies.

Nuclear Warfare in Antiquity?

Perhaps even more startling are passages in the **Mahabharata** that describe weapons of mass destruction with effects eerily similar to those of nuclear bombs. The texts speak of explosions brighter than a thousand suns, radioactive fallout, and the decimation of entire populations. One passage describes:

"A single projectile charged with all the power of the universe... An incandescent column of smoke and flame as bright as ten thousand suns rose in all its splendor... It was an unknown weapon, an iron thunderbolt, a gigantic messenger of death which reduced to ashes an entire race."

These descriptions have led some researchers to speculate that ancient civilizations may have possessed advanced weaponry. Notably, J. Robert Oppenheimer, often called the father of the atomic bomb, was familiar with these texts. After the first successful nuclear test in 1945, he famously quoted the **Bhagavad Gita**: "Now I am become Death, the destroyer of worlds." When asked in an interview whether this was the first atomic explosion, he cryptically replied, "Yes, in modern times."

Geological Evidence of Cataclysm

Beyond literary sources, there is geological evidence suggesting that catastrophic events reshaped the Earth's surface within human history. These events could account for the disappearance of continents like Kumari Kandam and the sudden decline of ancient civilizations.

The Great Extinctions

Approximately 11,500 years ago, at the end of the last Ice Age, Earth experienced a mass extinction event. Numerous large mammal species disappeared, and there were significant changes in climate and sea levels. Mainstream science often attributes these changes to gradual processes, but some researchers argue that they were the result of sudden cataclysms.

Allan and Delair, in their extensive work **Cataclysm!**, present evidence of rapid geological changes and massive flooding that could have submerged entire landmasses. They cite findings of vast lava fields, such as the Deccan Traps in India—a region covered by over 200,000 square miles of solidified lava. This suggests that intense volcanic activity could have been part of a global catastrophe.

Submerged Structures and Lost Cities

Advancements in marine archaeology have uncovered submerged structures off the coasts of India that may date back to periods when sea levels were significantly lower. Off the coast of Dwarka, in the Gulf of Cambay, researchers have discovered what appear to be the remains of ancient cities. Artifacts recovered from these sites have been carbon-dated to around 9500 BCE, predating known civilizations by millennia.

These discoveries lend credence to ancient accounts of lost cities and civilizations. If validated, they could rewrite our understanding of human history, placing advanced societies far earlier than currently accepted.

The Aryan Invasion Theory: A Misguided Narrative

Central to the suppression of India's ancient history is the Aryan Invasion Theory (AIT). Proposed in the 19th century, AIT suggested that Indo-European nomads invaded the Indian subcontinent around 1500 BCE, bringing with them the Vedic culture and Sanskrit language. This theory served to undermine India's indigenous heritage and fit the region's history into a Eurocentric framework.

Debunking the Aryan Myth

Modern scholarship has increasingly discredited the Aryan Invasion Theory. Archaeological evidence does not support the mass migrations or invasions proposed by the theory. Skeletal remains from the Indus Valley Civilization show continuity rather than abrupt change, indicating that the people of this civilization were indigenous.

Genetic studies have further challenged AIT. DNA analyses show deep genetic links between populations across the Indian subcontinent, dating back tens of thousands of years. These findings suggest that the development of Indian civilization was an internal process, not the result of external invasions.

The Saraswati River Civilization

Satellite imagery has revealed the dried-up course of the Saraswati River, often mentioned in the Rigveda, one of the oldest Indian texts. The river is believed to have been the cradle of the Vedic civilization. The decline of the Indus Valley Civilization may have been due to the drying up of this river rather than any invasion.

Recognizing the significance of the Saraswati River shifts the narrative. It emphasizes the continuity and antiquity of Indian civilization, undermining theories that place its origins in external influences.

Linguistic Connections and Global Influence

Language is a powerful tool for tracing cultural and historical connections. The prevalence of Sanskrit and Dravidian linguistic elements across various cultures suggests that ancient India may have had a more extensive influence than acknowledged.

Sanskrit: The Mother of Languages

Sanskrit is one of the oldest known languages and has influenced many modern tongues. Its complex grammar and vocabulary have led some linguists to consider it a foundational language for Indo-European languages.

Moreover, the presence of Sanskrit words and concepts in distant cultures raises questions about historical connections. For instance, similarities have been noted between Sanskrit and ancient Greek, Latin, and even Mayan languages. These links hint at cultural exchanges or shared origins that challenge the conventional timelines of human migration.

Tamil: A Proto-World Language?

Tamil, one of the world's oldest living languages, is rich in literature and historical records. Some researchers propose that Tamil may have been a proto-language that influenced or gave rise to other languages across Asia and the Pacific.

The discovery of similar scripts and linguistic patterns in places like Easter Island and among indigenous tribes in the Americas suggests that ancient Tamilians could have been seafarers who spread their culture widely. If true, this would significantly expand the recognized scope of ancient Indian influence.

Suppression and the Knowledge Filter

The reluctance to acknowledge these possibilities is not due to a lack of evidence but rather a persistent adherence to established paradigms. The knowledge filter operates by dismissing data that doesn't fit accepted theories, often labeling it as fringe or pseudo-science.

Ethnocentrism and Colonial Legacy

The colonial era left a lasting impact on how history is recorded and taught. European powers often portrayed colonized cultures as primitive or backward to justify their dominance. This ethnocentric view led to the dismissal of indigenous knowledge systems and historical accounts.

In India's case, the richness of its ancient texts and traditions was often overlooked or reinterpreted to fit Western narratives. The Aryan Invasion Theory is a prime example of how colonial powers imposed their frameworks onto the histories of others.

Scientific Materialism and Bias

Scientific materialism, the belief that only physical matter and observable phenomena are real, has dominated academic thought for centuries. While this approach has advanced our understanding in many areas, it can also limit perspectives.

Phenomena that don't fit within materialistic explanations are often ignored or ridiculed. This includes accounts of advanced ancient technologies, spiritual experiences, and other elements present in India's historical records. By dismissing these aspects, mainstream academia effectively suppresses alternative understandings of history.

Advancements in technology have provided tools to explore previously inaccessible areas. Underwater archaeology, satellite imaging, and genetic research offer new avenues to investigate ancient histories.

Collaboration across disciplines—combining archaeology, linguistics, genetics, and geology—can yield a more comprehensive understanding of the past. By integrating different fields of study, we can piece together the puzzle of human civilization's origins.

Respecting Indigenous Knowledge

Ancient cultures have preserved their histories through oral traditions, texts, and practices. These sources are invaluable for understanding the human journey. Respecting and studying indigenous knowledge systems can reveal insights that have been overlooked or undervalued.

In India's context, giving due consideration to Vedic texts, Tamil literature, and other ancient sources can illuminate aspects of history that have been neglected. This approach requires setting aside biases and acknowledging the legitimacy of non-Western perspectives.

Re-evaluating India's ancient history has profound implications. It challenges the linear progression model of civilization and suggests that advanced societies may have existed long before currently accepted timelines.

Advanced Ancient Civilizations

Accepting the possibility of advanced ancient civilizations raises questions about the capabilities of our ancestors. If they possessed knowledge of aeronautics, advanced metallurgy, and other sophisticated technologies, we must reconsider the trajectory of human development.

This perspective also opens the door to exploring how such knowledge was lost or suppressed over time. Understanding these patterns could help us preserve and rediscover valuable insights.

Recognizing the interconnectedness of ancient cultures emphasizes our shared human heritage. The spread of languages, technologies, and ideas across continents suggests that early civilizations were more interconnected than previously thought.

This understanding fosters a sense of global unity and can encourage collaborative efforts to uncover and preserve our collective history.

The Indian Mystery is not just about uncovering lost continents or deciphering ancient texts; it's about challenging the limitations imposed by outdated paradigms. India's rich heritage offers a gateway to reimagining human history, one that acknowledges the complexities and achievements of ancient civilizations.

Chapter 18: The China Mystery

In the early 20th century, a series of discoveries in China threatened to upend the established narratives of human evolution. Fossils unearthed from the depths of forgotten caves hinted at a complex tapestry of hominid life, one that defied the linear progression so comfortably accepted by the scientific elite.

This is the story of those discoveries—of Beijing Man and other finds that emerged from China's earth. It is a tale of ambition, rivalry, and the relentless pursuit of truth in the face of skepticism and suppression.

The Quest for Humanity's Origins Moves East

Following the contentious revelations of Java Man and the later debunked Piltdown Man, the scientific community found itself in disarray over the trajectory of human evolution. The fossils of *Pithecanthropus erectus* discovered by Eugène Dubois in Java had not secured unanimous support, and the Piltdown hoax only deepened the confusion. Researchers were eager for new evidence that could clarify the murky lineage of the Hominidae.

Many eyes turned toward China—a land rich in folklore and ancient artifacts, where the whispers of "dragon bones" had long intrigued Western scholars. These dragon bones, revered in traditional Chinese medicine and sold in apothecaries were in fact, fossils of prehistoric creatures. Among them, some believe might be the remains of early human ancestors.

The Unlikely Source: Dragon Bones and Early Clues

In 1900, German paleontologist Max Schlosser received a collection of fossils from Chinese drugstores, courtesy of Dr. K.

A. Haberer. Among the assortment of animal bones was a peculiar tooth from the Beijing area. Schlosser recognized it as a potential hominid molar—possibly belonging to a primitive human or an unknown species of ape. He suggested that China could be a promising ground for unearthing early human fossils, a notion that resonated with other scientists eager to solve the puzzle of human origins.

The Zhoukoudian Site: A Hidden Gold Mine

Gunnar Andersson, a Swedish geologist working with the Geological Survey of China, was among those captivated by Schlosser's suggestion. In 1918, Andersson visited Chicken Bone Hill (Chikushan) near the village of Zhoukoudian, approximately 40 kilometers southwest of Beijing. There, he observed a limestone quarry where fissures filled with red clay and fossilized bones hinted at ancient cave deposits.

By 1921, Andersson returned to the site with Otto Zdansky, an Austrian paleontologist, and Walter Granger from the American Museum of Natural History. Initial excavations yielded little significance—only recent fossils that did not satisfy their quest. However, local villagers guided Zdansky to another site near the Zhoukoudian railway station. Here, a similar limestone quarry presented red clay fissures teeming with fossilized remains.

It was at this secondary location that Andersson discovered fragments of quartz not native to the area. He posited that these pieces might be rudimentary tools, brought there by early hominids. Zdansky, however, was skeptical, dismissing the quartz fragments as naturally occurring debris rather than artifacts of human craftsmanship.

Despite their disagreements, Andersson was convinced that the site held the key to China's prehistoric past. He urged Zdansky to continue excavations, believing firmly that the remains of an ancient ancestor lay buried within the depths of the filled-in cave.

The First Hominid Evidence Emerges

Between 1921 and 1923, Zdansky conducted intermittent excavations at Zhoukoudian, albeit without great enthusiasm. His efforts eventually paid off when he uncovered two hominid teeth—a lower premolar and an upper molar. Tentatively dated to the Early Pleistocene, these teeth were significant yet remained unpublicized. Zdansky, for reasons unclear, chose not to announce his findings immediately, and the teeth were shipped to Sweden along with other fossils for further analysis.

It wasn't until 1926 that the teeth resurfaced in the scientific community. Professor Carl Wiman of Uppsala University, prompted by an upcoming visit from the Swedish Crown Prince, inquired if Zdansky had any noteworthy discoveries to showcase. The teeth from Zhoukoudian fit the bill, and their revelation reignited interest in China's potential contribution to understanding human evolution.

Gunnar Andersson presented the findings at a meeting in Beijing attended by the Crown Prince, declaring triumphantly that the ancient human he had predicted had indeed been found.

Davidson Black and the Birth of Sinanthropus

Among those present at the meeting was Davidson Black, a Canadian anatomist with a fervent interest in human evolution. Black had long held the belief that northern Asia was a cradle of early human development and had relocated to Beijing in pursuit of evidence to support his theory.

An Unwavering Vision

Born in 1884, Black graduated from the University of Toronto's medical school but was more drawn to anthropology than to practicing medicine. His fascination with human origins led him to accept a position at the Peking Union Medical College, funded by the Rockefeller Foundation. Despite the institution's focus on medical training, Black was determined to pursue paleoanthropological research.

Black's relentless lobbying for resources eventually paid off. After learning of the Zhoukoudian teeth, he collaborated with Andersson to secure funding from the Rockefeller Foundation for further excavations. The foundation, initially hesitant, was persuaded by Black's conviction and the allure of potentially groundbreaking discoveries.

The Unveiling of Beijing Man

Excavations resumed at Zhoukoudian in 1927, under challenging conditions exacerbated by China's civil unrest. Months passed with little to show for the effort. Morale waned among the team, but Black remained optimistic. His patience was rewarded when a single hominid tooth was unearthed. With this third tooth, Black felt confident enough to announce the discovery of a new genus, which he named *Sinanthropus pekinensis*—Peking Man.

Black's announcement was met with mixed reactions. While some hailed the discovery, others criticized the boldness of naming a new genus based on scant evidence. Undeterred, Black embarked on a campaign to promote his findings, traveling internationally to garner support and recognition. He met with skepticism but also with intrigue, managing to secure additional funding and resources.

A Treasure Unearthed

In December 1928, just as another excavation season was drawing to a close, a breakthrough occurred. Pei Wenzhong, a Chinese archaeologist working under Black's direction, discovered an almost complete skull cap of *Sinanthropus pekinensis*. The significance of this finding was monumental—it provided tangible evidence of a hominid species that could bridge gaps in the understanding of human evolution.

The skull exhibited a combination of primitive and advanced features. Its cranial capacity was larger than that of earlier hominids but smaller than that of modern humans. The pronounced brow ridges and other morphological characteristics suggested a being that stood somewhere between apes and humans.

Black's excitement knew no bounds. The discovery propelled him and the Zhoukoudian site into the international spotlight. The Rockefeller Foundation, now fully convinced of the importance of the work, established the Cenozoic Research Laboratory, ensuring continued financial and institutional support.

The Role of the Rockefeller Foundation

The transformation of the Rockefeller Foundation's involvement in paleoanthropology is a critical piece of this narrative. Initially focused on medical education and public health, the foundation's shift toward funding research into human origins was both strategic and ideological.

A Shift in Priorities

The early 20th century was a time of significant scientific advancement and exploration. The Rockefeller Foundation recognized the potential impact of groundbreaking discoveries in human evolution on broader societal and intellectual fronts. Funding research like Black's not only advanced scientific knowledge but also positioned the foundation at the forefront of influential academic and cultural movements.

Under the leadership of scientists like Max Mason, the foundation began to see the study of human origins as a means to understand and potentially guide human behavior. The notion was that by unraveling the mysteries of our past, we could better navigate our future—a concept that aligned with broader ambitions of social engineering and control prevalent among certain intellectual circles of the time.

Propaganda and Promotion

Black was astute in leveraging the foundation's resources not just for excavation but also for promoting his findings. He understood the importance of public perception and academic acceptance in solidifying *Sinanthropus*' place in the scientific community.

He orchestrated a strategic publicity campaign, enlisting the support of prominent figures like Sir Grafton Elliot Smith, an influential anatomist and anthropologist. Together, they worked to generate excitement and legitimacy around Beijing Man, presenting it as a pivotal piece in the puzzle of human evolution.

This concerted effort paid off. The discoveries at Zhoukoudian became celebrated milestones, and Black secured his legacy as a key figure in paleoanthropology. The Rockefeller Foundation's backing was instrumental in this success, illustrating how financial and institutional support can shape scientific narratives.

Controversies and Conundrums at Zhoukoudian

Despite the fanfare, the Zhoukoudian site was not without its controversies. As excavations continued, questions arose about the interpretation of the findings, the methodology employed, and the implications for the established timelines of human evolution.

The Fire Debate

One of the significant points of contention was the presence—or absence—of evidence for the controlled use of fire by *Sinanthropus pekinensis*. Early reports by Black and his team made no mention of ash layers or hearths, which would suggest that these hominids had mastered fire—a hallmark of advanced cognitive and cultural development.

However, in 1931, French archaeologist Henri Breuil reported extensive ash deposits and a multitude of stone tools at the site. This raised eyebrows: how could such prominent features have been overlooked by the earlier excavators?

Black and his colleagues offered explanations, claiming they had noticed signs of fire and tools but had been uncertain of their significance or hesitant to report them without definitive proof. Critics, however, suggested that the initial omission might have been deliberate. Acknowledging the use of fire and sophisticated tools could imply that *Sinanthropus* was more advanced than previously thought, potentially disrupting the neatly constructed evolutionary hierarchy.

The Cannibalism Hypothesis

Further fueling the debate were the observations made by Franz Weidenreich, who succeeded Black after his untimely death in 1934. Weidenreich noted peculiarities in the hominid skulls recovered from Zhoukoudian—many were missing their base, and some bore marks that suggested deliberate breaking.

He proposed that these signs pointed to ritualistic cannibalism, with *Sinanthropus* individuals consuming their kind. This notion was both sensational and unsettling, casting Beijing Man in a primitive and brutal light.

Alternatively, some scholars posited that the skulls might have been brought into the cave by predators or that the damage resulted from natural processes. The idea that a more advanced hominid species could have preyed upon *Sinanthropus* was also considered, adding another layer of complexity to the interpretation of the site.

Morphological Dating and Its Pitfalls

A significant methodological issue that emerged from the Zhoukoudian findings—and from other sites in China—was the practice of "morphological dating." This approach involved assigning ages to hominid fossils based primarily on their physical characteristics rather than on stratigraphy or other more objective dating methods.

In the case of Zhoukoudian, the argument was made that the cranial capacity of *Sinanthropus* increased over time, suggesting evolutionary progression. Wu Rukang and Lin Shenglong, writing in *Scientific American* in 1983, claimed that the earliest skull had a capacity of 915 cubic centimeters, while later skulls averaged

1,075 cubic centimeters, with the most recent at 1,140 cubic centimeters.

However, this assertion was misleading. The earliest skull with the smallest cranial capacity belonged to a child—a fact conveniently omitted. Moreover, some skulls from earlier layers had larger capacities than those from higher layers, undermining the supposed trend.

Relying on morphological dating allows preconceived notions about evolution to dictate the interpretation of evidence. It creates a circular logic where fossils are dated based on their expected place in the evolutionary timeline, which in turn is used to support that very timeline.

The Disappearance of the Original Fossils

Adding to the mystery and controversy was the disappearance of the original *Sinanthropus* fossils. As World War II loomed, efforts were made to safeguard the precious remains. In 1941, the fossils were packed into crates intended to be shipped to the United States for protection.

Tragically, the crates never made it out of China. The outbreak of war and the subsequent chaos resulted in the loss of the fossils, which have never been recovered. This loss has had profound implications for the study of Beijing Man. Researchers have since had to rely on casts, notes, and secondary materials, limiting the ability to conduct new analyses with modern techniques.

The absence of the original specimens has fueled speculation and debate, with some questioning the validity of earlier interpretations and others lamenting the lost opportunity to apply advances in dating and genetic analysis.

Reassessing the Evolutionary Narrative

The discoveries in China, while groundbreaking, also highlight the challenges inherent in reconstructing human evolution. The evidence from Zhoukoudian and other sites does not fit neatly into a linear progression from ape-like ancestors to modern humans. Instead, it suggests a complex and possibly contemporaneous coexistence of various hominid species.

Overlapping Hominids in the Pleistocene

In several locations across China, fossils attributed to different hominid species have been found in strata that suggest overlapping periods. For instance:

- **Lantian Man**: Discovered in Shaanxi province, these remains are considered to be primitive *Homo erectus*. Faunal evidence and paleomagnetic dating place them within a range that overlaps with Zhoukoudian.
- **Tongzi Man**: Fossils found in Guizhou province, identified as *Homo sapiens*, were associated with fauna typical of the Middle Pleistocene—a period also attributed to *Homo erectus* sites.
- **Maba Man:** A skull exhibiting a mix of modern human and Neanderthal features was found in Guangdong province, again within Middle Pleistocene contexts.

These findings challenge the notion that one hominid species necessarily evolved into another in a strict sequence. The possibility that multiple hominid species coexisted complicates the evolutionary narrative and suggests a more intricate web of human ancestry.

The Problem with Morphological Dating

The practice of morphological dating becomes particularly problematic in this context. By assigning ages to fossils based on their perceived evolutionary advancement, scientists risk introducing bias and circular reasoning into their conclusions.

For example, if a *Homo sapiens* fossil is found in the Middle Pleistocene strata, but prevailing theories dictate that modern humans did not exist at that time, researchers might adjust the dating of the strata or propose that the fossil is intrusive from a later period. This approach dismisses the possibility that modern humans could have existed earlier than currently accepted.

Such methodological issues highlight the need for more rigorous and objective dating techniques and for openness to revising established timelines in light of new evidence.

Suppression and Selective Acceptance of Evidence

Throughout the history of paleoanthropology, there have been instances where evidence that does not fit the accepted paradigm is downplayed or ignored. The emphasis on promoting findings that support the prevailing theories can lead to a biased understanding of human evolution.

In the case of China, the desire to find a linear progression of hominid development may have influenced the interpretation of the evidence. Contradictory findings, such as the possible coexistence of *Homo erectus* and *Homo sapiens*, challenge the simplicity of the established model.

The Broader Implications

The China Mystery is not just about fossils and ancient bones; it is a reflection of how science, ideology, and cultural perspectives intertwine. The interpretation of archaeological and paleontological evidence is influenced by the beliefs and expectations of the researchers, as well as by the institutions that fund and support their work.

Scientific Objectivity and Bias

True scientific inquiry requires a willingness to follow the evidence wherever it leads, even if it contradicts long-held beliefs. The tendency to fit data into existing frameworks can hinder the advancement of knowledge.

Acknowledging and addressing biases—whether conscious or unconscious—is crucial. This includes being open to alternative explanations and being cautious about relying too heavily on assumptions derived from current theories.

The Role of Funding and Institutional Support

The involvement of powerful organizations like the Rockefeller Foundation demonstrates how funding can shape scientific research. While financial support is essential for conducting extensive studies, it can also influence the focus and interpretation of the research.

Institutions may have agendas or priorities that align with certain outcomes, consciously or unconsciously guiding researchers toward conclusions that support those aims. This underscores the importance of transparency and independence in scientific endeavors.

This perspective opens up new avenues of inquiry. How did these different hominid species influence each other? What does this mean for our understanding of human adaptability, migration, and cultural development?

The story of Beijing Man and the other hominid finds in China is a testament to the complexity of unraveling our past. It challenges us to question assumptions, scrutinize methodologies, and remain open to possibilities that may disrupt conventional wisdom.

Part IV: The Forbidden History of the Body

The human body is a marvel of evolution—a complex system that has fascinated, perplexed, and often terrified humanity since the dawn of consciousness. Yet, throughout history, much of what pertains to our physical selves has been cloaked in taboo, shrouded by cultural norms, religious edicts, and societal fears. This has led to a fragmented understanding of our biology and the forces that drive us, leaving critical aspects of the human experience buried beneath layers of suppression and misinformation.

In this section, we embark on an illuminating journey to uncover the hidden narratives that have shaped our relationship with our bodies. We'll delve into the **Forbidden History of Attraction**, exploring the psychological and biological mechanisms that draw individuals together—mechanisms that have been both celebrated and censored across different eras and cultures. Moving into the **Forbidden History of Sex**, we'll confront the stigmas and secret knowledge surrounding human sexuality, examining how science and society have alternately suppressed and exploited this fundamental aspect of human life.

Food, a basic necessity for survival, carries its clandestine past. The **Forbidden History of Food** will reveal how power structures have manipulated diets and access to nourishment, influencing health and social hierarchies in ways that persist today. In the **Forbidden History of Surgical Instrument/Medicine**, we'll uncover how medical knowledge has been controlled, often withheld from those who need it most, and the impact this has had on human longevity and well-being.

Backed by scientific research and interdisciplinary studies, this exploration challenges long-held beliefs and exposes the systemic efforts to control knowledge about our bodies. By shedding light on these forbidden histories, we aim not only to inform but to empower—a call to reclaim the narrative of our physical existence from the shadows of ignorance and into the clarity of understanding.

Chapter 19: The Forbidden History of Attraction

Attraction—a force so potent it has toppled empires, ignited wars, and shaped the course of human history. Yet, despite its overwhelming influence, the true nature of attraction remains shrouded in mystery, distorted by myths, and suppressed by societal norms that fear its raw power. Today, we're tearing down the veil to expose the forbidden history of attraction, revealing truths that will challenge everything you thought you knew about desire, connection, and the irresistible pull between individuals.

A Bold Question: What Makes Someone Irresistible?

Let's cut through the noise. What genuinely makes a person attractive? Is it the sculpted physique chiseled by hours at the gym? The flashing of wealth through expensive cars and designer clothes? Or perhaps it's something far more profound, an intangible essence that can't be bought or faked. The uncomfortable truth is that attraction isn't about superficial attributes. It's about behaviors and attitudes—core elements that can be cultivated and mastered.

Consider this: Throughout history, legendary figures known for their allure weren't always the wealthiest or the most physically imposing. Take Don Juan, the infamous seducer whose name is synonymous with irresistible charm. What set him apart wasn't his bank account or his looks; it was something else entirely. And here's the kicker—you can learn these traits. Yes, you read that right. The qualities that make someone magnetic can be developed, honed, and wielded to transform your interactions.

Deconstructing Attraction: Beyond the Surface

If you've ever watched someone who's naturally captivating, you'll notice certain patterns. First, they're genuinely engaged in the moment. They're not anxiously checking their phone or scanning the room for someone "better." They exude confidence without arrogance, making those around them feel both at ease and intrigued.

Second, they lead interactions with a subtle but unmistakable command. They aren't domineering, but they set the tone and direction of the conversation. Their decisiveness is alluring, signaling a sense of purpose and direction.

Third, they listen—listen. In a world where everyone is desperate to be heard, giving someone your full attention is a rare and precious gift. It makes the other person feel valued and important, which, in turn, draws them closer to you.

These behaviors aren't innate gifts bestowed upon a lucky few at birth. They're skills—learned, practiced, and perfected over time. The problem is, that society often discourages us from embracing these traits. We're told to be humble to the point of diminishing ourselves, to avoid taking the lead for fear of appearing aggressive, and to hold back our true selves to fit into neat, acceptable boxes.

The Evolutionary Purpose of Attraction: Nature's Survival Mechanism

Let's get something straight. Attraction isn't just a social construct or a frivolous game. It's a fundamental component of human evolution. For millennia, our ancestors relied on attraction to select mates who would enhance their chances of survival and the propagation of their genes. Women, in particular, developed a keen sense for behaviors that signaled a man's ability to provide, protect, and persevere.

Think about it. In the harsh realities of early human existence, physical strength and resources mattered, but so did courage, decisiveness, and the ability to remain calm under pressure. These traits indicated that a man could handle threats, secure food, and ensure the safety of his family.

Fast forward to today, and while the environment has changed drastically, our biological instincts haven't caught up. Women are still subconsciously drawn to these primal signals of a man's suitability as a partner.

The Myth of Materialism: Why Money and Looks Aren't Enough

Modern culture bombards us with the idea that wealth and physical appearance are the ultimate keys to attraction. Buy this car, wear this brand, get those abs—and you'll have people falling at your feet. But let's face reality. How many times have you seen someone who has all these things and still struggles in their relationships? The reason is simple: attraction isn't transactional.

Don Juan didn't have access to modern luxuries, yet his allure was legendary. His secret wasn't in flaunting assets but in embodying qualities that resonated on a deeper level. He was confident but not cocky, assertive but not aggressive, and he genuinely appreciated the company of women—not just for physical gratification but for meaningful connection.

The Legend of Don Juan: Separating Myth from Mastery

To understand the forbidden history of attraction, we must dissect the figure of Don Juan. Often vilified as a mere womanizer, the essence of his character is misunderstood. Don Juan was a master of social dynamics, a man who navigated the complexities of human interaction with finesse.

He didn't rely on manipulative tactics or deceit. Instead, he was authentic, living by his code and principles. He was unashamed of his desires yet respected the autonomy of those he engaged with. This balance is crucial. It's not about conquest but about connection.

Don Juan's ability to attract wasn't about exerting power over others but about harnessing his inner strength. He was comfortable in his skin, embraced his circumstances—no matter how dire—and always acted with intention. These are the traits that made him irresistible, and they're just as potent today.

The Modern Misconception: The Rise of the 'Nice Guy' Syndrome

In stark contrast to the confident allure of figures like Don Juan, today's society often promotes a misguided notion of attraction. Men are encouraged to be overly accommodating, to suppress their own needs and desires in favor of pleasing others. This "Nice Guy" syndrome leads to frustration and resentment when the expected reciprocation doesn't materialize.

Here's the hard truth: being overly nice isn't the same as being genuinely kind or respectful. It's a façade that lacks authenticity and undermines self-respect. Women—and people in general—can sense this dissonance. It doesn't inspire attraction; it breeds indifference or even contempt.

The Cost of Suppressing Authenticity: A Case Study in Unattractive Behavior

Consider the all-too-common scenario of the man who, in an attempt to win affection, abandons his interests, opinions, and boundaries. He agrees with everything, avoids any form of conflict, and becomes a chameleon in hopes of being liked. But this strategy backfires spectacularly.

By not asserting himself, he signals a lack of confidence and self-worth. Attraction fades because there's nothing substantial to connect with. Remember, attraction is about magnetism, and magnets need opposing forces to draw together. A person without their own identity cannot create that dynamic.

Embracing the Forbidden Traits: Reclaiming the Essence of Attraction

So, what are the forbidden traits that society doesn't want you to embrace? They are confidence without arrogance, assertiveness without aggression, authenticity without apology, and a purpose-driven approach to life.

These traits are often suppressed because they challenge the status quo. A confident, self-assured individual is harder to manipulate. They make decisions that align with their values, not societal pressures. This autonomy is threatening to structures that rely on conformity.

But here's the kicker—embracing these traits not only enhances personal relationships but also leads to a more fulfilling life. It's about being the protagonist of your own story rather than a background character in someone else's.

Actionable Strategies: Cultivating Irresistible Qualities

1. **Develop Genuine Confidence**: Confidence isn't about bravado; it's about self-assurance rooted in competence. Pursue skills and knowledge that enhance your abilities. Set and achieve personal goals to build a solid foundation of self-belief.
2. **Embrace Authenticity**: Stop trying to be what others expect. Define your values and standards. Authenticity is magnetic because it's rare. People are drawn to those who are unapologetically themselves.
3. **Practice Assertiveness**: Learn to express your thoughts and desires openly and respectfully. Being assertive shows that you value yourself and are willing to stand up for what you believe in.
4. **Listen Actively**: Shift your focus from trying to impress to genuinely engaging with others. Listening builds rapport and demonstrates respect. It also allows you to connect on a deeper level.
5. **Lead with Purpose**: Have a clear direction in life. Whether it's personal goals, professional ambitions, or passions, a sense of purpose is attractive. It shows that

you're going somewhere and invites others to join you on the journey.

6. **Stay Composed Under Pressure**: Life is unpredictable. How you handle challenges speaks volumes about your character. Remaining calm and decisive in tough situations is not only effective but also highly attractive.

The Evolutionary Echo: Why These Traits Matter

These strategies aren't just social hacks; they're deeply rooted in our evolutionary psychology. Throughout history, individuals who exhibited these traits were more likely to succeed and, therefore, more likely to attract mates.

Confidence signals the ability to handle challenges. Authenticity indicates reliability. Assertiveness suggests the capability of securing resources. Purpose demonstrates direction and the potential for providing stability. These are the subconscious cues that trigger attraction on a primal level.

The Pitfalls to Avoid: Learning from Modern Missteps

In contrast to these empowering traits, some behaviors are guaranteed to repel. Neediness, desperation, and entitlement are major turn-offs. They indicate a lack of self-sufficiency and emotional maturity.

For example, the man who constantly seeks validation from others undermines his value. Or the individual who feels entitled to someone's affection without earning it through meaningful connection. These attitudes not only sabotage personal relationships but also erode self-respect.

Rewriting the Narrative: Moving Beyond Societal Constraints

It's time to challenge the narratives that limit personal growth and authentic connections. Society often promotes superficial measures of worth—appearance, wealth, social status—while discouraging the development of deeper, more substantial qualities.

By focusing on cultivating genuine traits that enhance attraction, you not only improve your interpersonal relationships but also contribute to a culture that values authenticity over façade.

Here's the ultimate secret: attraction starts from within. It's not about external validation or meeting arbitrary standards. It's about becoming the best version of yourself and letting that radiate outward.

When you prioritize personal growth, embrace your authentic self, and live with purpose, you naturally attract others. It's a byproduct, not the primary goal. This shift in mindset is powerful. It frees you from the exhausting pursuit of approval and allows you to focus on what truly matters.

Don't let societal expectations dictate who you should be. The forbidden history of attraction teaches us that true magnetism comes from embracing qualities that are often suppressed or overlooked. It's time to reclaim these traits and, in doing so, unlock a new level of connection and fulfillment.

Start today. Assess where you are and where you want to be. Commit to personal growth, not for the sake of others but for yourself. As you transform, you'll find that not only does your personal life improve, but you also inspire others to embark on their journeys.

Attraction is a powerful force—one that has shaped the course of history and continues to influence our lives in profound ways. By understanding and embracing its true nature, we tap into a wellspring of potential that goes far beyond personal relationships.

The forbidden history of attraction isn't about manipulation or superficial tactics. It's about authenticity, confidence, and living with intention. These are the qualities that have made figures like

Don Juan legendary, not because of their conquests but because of their mastery over themselves.

Embrace the forbidden. Unleash your true self. The world is waiting.

Chapter 20: The Forbidden History of Sex & Romantic Relationships

Sexuality has always been a powerful force in human society—a force that shapes cultures, ignites revolutions, and, paradoxically, often remains shrouded in taboo. The history of sex and romantic relationships is not just a chronicle of human intimacy but a battleground of control, oppression, and liberation. This chapter delves into the suppressed narratives, the deliberate erasures, and the societal constructs that have kept the true history of human sexuality hidden from view.

The Cloaked Anatomy: Rediscovering Female Pleasure

For centuries, the female body has been a subject of fascination and fear, leading to a systematic suppression of knowledge about female sexuality. At the heart of this suppression lies the clitoris—a small organ with a singular purpose: sexual pleasure. Despite its significance, myths and misconceptions about its anatomy have persisted, not only among the general populace but also within the medical community.

The Elusive Organ: A History of Denial and Rediscovery

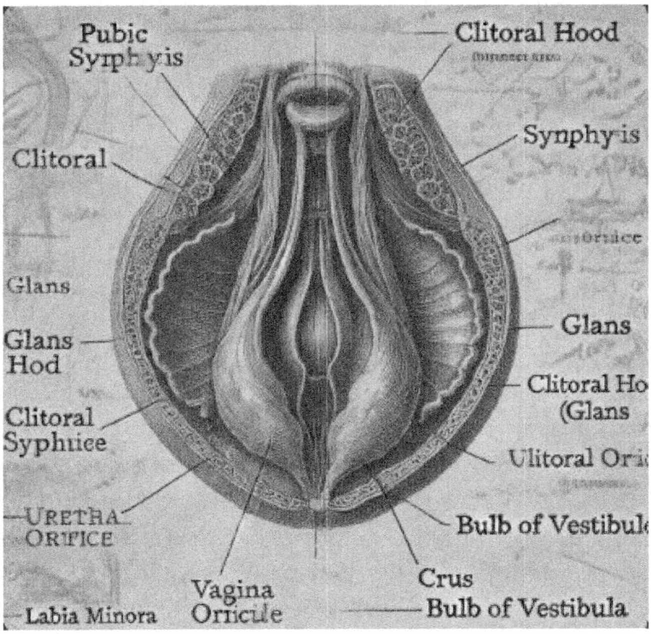

The earliest recorded mention of the clitoris dates back to ancient Greece. Hippocrates, the father of modern medicine, referred to it as the "little pillar." However, this knowledge was not passed down unchallenged. By the time of the Roman Empire, prominent physicians like Galen dismissed the existence of the clitoris altogether, plunging it into obscurity.

The Renaissance brought a renewed interest in human anatomy, yet the clitoris remained controversial. In 16th-century Europe, anatomists like Charles Estienne acknowledged its existence but labeled it the "shameful member," reflecting the deep-seated misogyny of the era. Others, such as Realdo Colombo and Gabriele Falloppio, claimed to have discovered it anew, each asserting ownership over the knowledge as if it were a groundbreaking revelation.

Despite these periodic "discoveries," the clitoris was repeatedly erased from medical texts. Notably, in the 1947 edition of "Gray's Anatomy," one of the most authoritative medical references, the clitoris was omitted entirely. This pattern of recognition followed by denial illustrates a persistent discomfort with female sexual autonomy.

Modern Medicine's Blind Spot

It wasn't until the late 20th and early 21st centuries that the clitoris began to receive proper scientific attention. Urologist Helen O'Connell utilized MRI technology to map its full anatomy, revealing that the external glans is just the tip of a much larger, complex structure. Her work confirmed what some 19th-century anatomists had observed but was largely forgotten or ignored.

However, even with modern imaging and research, medical education has been slow to integrate this knowledge. Obstetrics and gynecology often focus on reproductive functions, neglecting aspects of female pleasure. Surgical practices during childbirth, such as episiotomies performed at specific angles, risk damaging the clitoral structures without fully understanding the consequences.

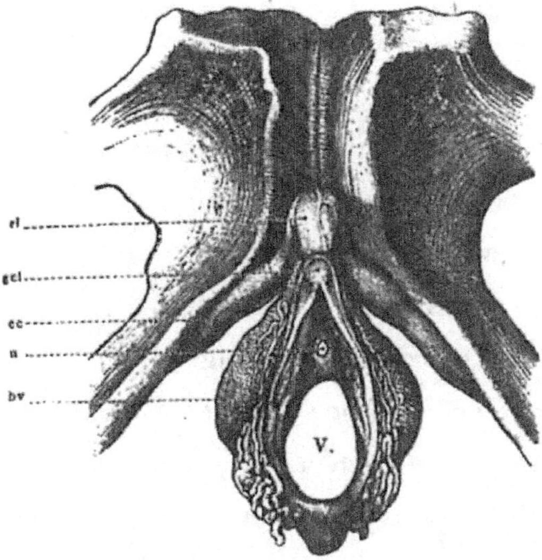

Clitoris and vestibular bulbs. From Georg Ludwi
Kobelt 1844 *Die Männlichen und Weiblichen Wollusts-Organe des Menschen und Einiger Saugetiere.*

The Politics of Female Sexuality

The suppression of knowledge about the clitoris is emblematic of a broader societal discomfort with female sexuality. Throughout history, patriarchal structures have sought to control women's bodies, often through moralistic and pseudoscientific means.

Medical Misogyny and Cultural Taboo

In the 19th and early 20th centuries, medical professionals pathologized female sexuality. Conditions like "hysteria" were diagnosed with alarming frequency, leading to invasive treatments, including clitoridectomies performed without consent. Physicians like Isaac Baker-Brown advocated for these procedures, claiming to cure women of various psychological ailments by removing their capacity for sexual pleasure.

Such practices were not limited to fringe medical theories but were endorsed by established institutions. The underlying motive was clear: to suppress women's autonomy and enforce strict moral codes that kept them subservient.

Freud's Misguided Influence

Sigmund Freud's theories further complicated the understanding of female sexuality. He posited that clitoral orgasms were "immature" and that women should achieve "mature" sexuality through vaginal orgasms. This idea not only invalidated women's experiences but also reinforced the notion that female pleasure should be tied directly to male sexual performance.

Freud's influence permeated Western thought, shaping attitudes toward women's sexuality for decades. It contributed to a culture where discussions of the clitoris were marginalized, and women's sexual satisfaction was deemed unimportant.

The Social Consequences of Ignorance

The deliberate suppression of knowledge about female anatomy and sexuality has had profound social implications. It has affected medical practices, educational curricula, and personal relationships, perpetuating cycles of misunderstanding and dissatisfaction.

Educational Failures

Sex education, where it exists, often omits critical information about female anatomy. This gap leaves generations of individuals ill-equipped to understand their bodies or those of their partners. The myth of the "elusive clitoris" persists, reinforcing harmful stereotypes about women's sexuality being mysterious or unknowable.

Furthermore, the lack of comprehensive education contributes to unhealthy attitudes toward sex, fostering environments where consent and communication are not adequately emphasized.

Medical Negligence

In medical contexts, the oversight extends beyond childbirth practices. Women's reports of sexual dysfunction or discomfort are frequently dismissed or inadequately addressed. The medical community's historical bias has led to a deficit in research on female sexual health, resulting in fewer treatment options and less understanding of common issues.

Moreover, conditions like endometriosis and polycystic ovary syndrome (PCOS) are often underdiagnosed, in part due to a lack of emphasis on women's health concerns that do not directly relate to reproduction.

Reclaiming Female Sexuality

Despite centuries of suppression, women have continually sought to reclaim control over their bodies and sexuality. The feminist movements of the 20th and 21st centuries have made significant strides in challenging patriarchal narratives and advocating for sexual liberation.

The Rise of Sexual Empowerment

The sexual revolution of the 1960s and 1970s marked a turning point. Women began openly discussing their desires, advocating for reproductive rights, and challenging traditional gender roles. Publications like "Our Bodies, Ourselves" provided accessible information about female anatomy and health, empowering women with knowledge long denied to them.

In recent years, movements like #MeToo have brought issues of consent and sexual agency to the forefront, highlighting the ongoing struggle against systemic sexism and abuse.

Medical Advancements and Advocacy

The work of researchers like Helen O'Connell has reignited interest in female sexual health within the medical community. There is a growing recognition of the need for gender-specific research and a more nuanced understanding of women's health issues.

Advocacy groups and organizations are pushing for comprehensive sex education, better medical training, and increased funding for research into female sexuality. These efforts aim to dismantle the lingering taboos and promote a more inclusive and informed society.

The Intersection of Race, Gender, and Sexuality

The suppression of female sexuality is further complicated when considering intersections with race and class. Women of color have faced additional layers of marginalization, with their bodies often hypersexualized or devalued in societal narratives.

Historical Exploitation

Throughout history, women of color have been subjected to exploitation and abuse under the guise of scientific inquiry or colonial conquest. The case of Saartjie Baartman, known as the "Hottentot Venus," exemplifies this tragic reality. Displayed in 19th-century Europe as a curiosity due to her physique, Baartman's body was objectified and dissected, symbolizing the dehumanization of Black women.

Such instances highlight how racism and sexism intersect to deny certain groups agency over their bodies and narratives.

Contemporary Challenges

Today, women of color continue to battle stereotypes and systemic barriers that affect their sexual health and autonomy. Disparities in healthcare access, cultural stigmas, and socioeconomic factors contribute to unequal treatment and outcomes.

Recognizing and addressing these intersections is crucial for a holistic understanding of the forbidden history of sex and romantic relationships.

The Role of Media and Culture

Media representations have played a significant role in shaping societal attitudes toward sex and relationships. From literature to film, the portrayal of sexuality often reflects and reinforces prevailing taboos and biases.

Censorship and Sensationalism

In many cultures, discussions of sex have been deemed inappropriate for public discourse, leading to censorship and self-censorship among creators. When sexual content does appear, it is frequently sensationalized, focusing on titillation rather than authentic representation.

This dichotomy contributes to a distorted understanding of sexuality, where it is either hidden away or exploited for entertainment, without genuine engagement with its complexities.

Breaking the Silence

Artists and writers have often challenged these norms, using their work to explore and expose the realities of human sexuality. Literary figures like Anaïs Nin and D.H. Lawrence faced controversy for their candid depictions of desire and intimacy.

In cinema, films that address sexual themes with nuance and depth have pushed boundaries and sparked important conversations. However, such works frequently encounter resistance, highlighting the persistent discomfort society holds toward open discussions of sex.

Legal and Ethical Dimensions

The regulation of sexual behavior extends into the legal realm, where laws have historically been used to control and punish certain expressions of sexuality.

Criminalization and Control

Throughout history, various forms of sexual activity have been criminalized, often rooted in moral or religious doctrines. Laws against homosexuality, adultery, and other consensual acts have been used to police private behavior and enforce conformity.

These legal restrictions disproportionately affect marginalized groups, reinforcing power structures and perpetuating injustice.

Movements for Reform

Legal challenges and advocacy have led to significant changes in many parts of the world. The decriminalization of homosexuality, the recognition of marital rape, and the legalization of same-sex marriage are milestones achieved through relentless activism.

These advances demonstrate the capacity for societies to evolve and embrace more equitable understandings of human rights and dignity.

The forbidden history of sex and romantic relationships is a testament to the enduring struggle between oppressive forces and the innate human desire for connection and pleasure.

Understanding this history is not merely an academic exercise but a crucial step toward dismantling the lingering taboos and misconceptions that hinder genuine intimacy and equality. It calls us to question the structures that have dictated norms and to advocate for a future where knowledge is accessible, bodies are respected, and love is free from the chains of prejudice.

Chapter 21: The Forbidden History of Food

Food is more than sustenance; it's a powerful symbol woven into the fabric of human culture, religion, and history. Across civilizations, what we consume—or choose not to consume—has been dictated by a complex interplay of beliefs, taboos, and societal norms. The forbidden foods of our past reveal a hidden narrative about humanity's fears, desires, and the lengths we'll go to enforce conformity. This chapter delves into the clandestine history of prohibited foods, unearthing the startling truths that have been buried beneath layers of tradition and dogma.

The Sacred Act of Eating: More Than Just a Meal

From the earliest days of human civilization, eating has been imbued with spiritual significance. Religious ceremonies often revolve around food, transforming ordinary meals into sacred rituals. In many traditions, consuming certain foods is a way to commune with the divine, while abstaining from others serves as a test of faith.

Food Taboos as Social Glue

Religious dietary laws have historically served to unify followers and set them apart from outsiders. By dictating what is permissible to eat, these laws create a shared identity and foster a sense of community. For instance, the kosher laws in Judaism and halal guidelines in Islam are not merely about health or hygiene; they are profound expressions of religious obedience and cultural identity.

Below are some forbidden foods and what they are said to represent…

1. **The Jewish Pig: A Symbol of Hatred and Misunderstanding**

Perhaps no animal has been more maligned due to religious dietary laws than the pig. In Jewish and Islamic traditions, pork is strictly forbidden. This prohibition has, over centuries, been twisted into grotesque stereotypes and used as a tool for persecution.

Antisemitism and the Pig Symbolism

During the Middle Ages, the image of the "Judensau" or "Jew's sow" emerged in Europe. This derogatory depiction showed Jewish people in obscene contact with pigs, serving as a visual propaganda tool to dehumanize and vilify them. Such imagery reinforced hateful narratives and justified discrimination, culminating in some of the darkest chapters of human history.

The Spanish Inquisition's Culinary Witch Hunt

In 15th-century Spain, food became a weapon in the hands of the Inquisition. Converted Jews and Muslims, known as "conversos" and "Moriscos," were closely monitored for signs of heresy. One of the telltale signs? Their eating habits.

2. **Adafina: The Stew That Could Get You Killed**

Traditional dishes like adafina, a slow-cooked stew prepared by Jews for the Sabbath, became evidence of secret adherence to Judaism. The mere act of cooking this meal could lead to accusations of heresy and a death sentence. Food, in this context, was not just sustenance but a marker of identity that could mean the difference between life and death.

The Kosher Conundrum: Complexity and Controversy

Jewish dietary laws, or kashrut, are among the most detailed and complex in the world. These laws go beyond simple prohibitions, encompassing intricate rules about food preparation and consumption.

Defining Kosher in a Modern World

The challenge of maintaining kosher practices in contemporary society has led to legal debates and differing interpretations. In some places, the government has been called upon to define what constitutes kosher food, raising questions about the separation of church and state.

Human ingenuity shines in the creative ways people have found to navigate their dietary laws. When confronted with prohibitions, cultures often develop substitutes or reinterpretations to maintain their culinary traditions.

3. Disguised Dishes and Semantic Maneuvers

In medieval Europe, during periods of fasting like Lent, Christians were forbidden from eating meat. Chefs responded by creating dishes that looked and tasted like meat but were made from fish or vegetables. Similarly, some Buddhist monks have reclassified certain meats as permissible based on technicalities, reflecting a universal tendency to bend rules without outright breaking them.

4. The Eucharist Divide: Bread That Split the Church

The type of bread used in the Christian Eucharist—leavened or unleavened—became a major point of contention between the Eastern Orthodox and Roman Catholic Churches. This seemingly small difference contributed to the Great Schism of 1054, which split Christianity into two major branches.

The symbolism of Leavened vs. Unleavened Bread

For the Eastern Orthodox Church, leavened bread symbolized the risen Christ, while the Roman Catholic Church used unleavened bread to reflect the purity and simplicity of Jesus' sacrifice. The dispute over bread types underscores how food can embody profound theological differences.

5. Dogs on the Menu: Cultural Relativism and Moral Outrage

The consumption of dog meat is a practice that elicits strong emotional reactions, especially in Western societies where dogs are considered companions. However, in various cultures around the world, dog meat has been a traditional source of nutrition.

The Clash of Cultural Norms

When immigrants bring their culinary traditions to new countries, conflicts can arise. In the 1980s, reports of dog meat consumption among certain Asian communities in the United States sparked legal debates and public outrage. This tension highlights the challenges of cultural relativism and the complexities of imposing one society's moral framework onto another.

6. **Holy Cow: The Sacred Bovine in India**

In India, the cow is not just an animal but a sacred symbol deeply embedded in Hinduism. The veneration of cows has significant social and economic implications, influencing dietary practices and even inciting conflict.

The Economics of Reverence

Despite widespread poverty and hunger, cows in India often roam free and are protected from slaughter. This paradox can be perplexing to outsiders but makes sense within the cultural and religious context that values the cow as a symbol of life and fertility.

7. **The Maasai and Their Cattle: A Bond Beyond the Material**

For the Maasai people of East Africa, cattle are more than livestock—they are the cornerstone of their culture, economy, and spirituality. The Maasai's relationship with their cattle illustrates how food sources can be integral to a community's identity.

Blood and Milk: Dietary Staples

The Maasai diet traditionally consists of cow's milk and blood, reflecting a harmonious relationship with their animals. This practice underscores a form of sustenance that is sustainable and respectful, blurring the lines between nourishment and reverence.

8. The Vegetarian Ideal: Utopian Dreams and Harsh Realities

Vegetarianism has often been linked to moral and spiritual purity. From ancient philosophers to modern activists, the choice to abstain from meat is frequently presented as a path to a more ethical and enlightened existence.

The Paradox of Violent Vegetarians

History reveals that abstaining from meat does not necessarily correlate with non-violence. Notably, some infamous leaders who endorsed vegetarianism, like Adolf Hitler, were responsible for unimaginable atrocities. This contradiction challenges the assumption that dietary choices alone can define moral character.

9. Jainism: The Extreme Pursuit of Non-Violence

Jainism, an ancient Indian religion, takes the principle of non-violence to its utmost expression. Jains follow strict dietary laws that prohibit harm to any living creature, extending even to microorganisms.

The Ethics of Consumption

Jains avoid root vegetables like potatoes and onions because harvesting them can kill the entire plant and disturb organisms in the soil. This meticulous attention to the impact of food choices exemplifies an extreme commitment to non-violence but also raises questions about practicality and sustainability.

10. Foie Gras: Culinary Delight or Ethical Dilemma?

Foie gras, a luxury food product made from the liver of a specially fattened duck or goose, has become a focal point in debates over animal rights and culinary tradition.

Tradition vs. Compassion

While some argue that foie gras is a cultural heritage that must be preserved, others decry the methods used to produce it as inhumane. The controversy highlights the tension between maintaining gastronomic traditions and evolving ethical standards.

11. The Fiery Allure of Chili Peppers: Pain as Pleasure

Chili peppers have a storied history of being both feared and revered. Their capacity to induce pain and pleasure simultaneously has made them a subject of fascination and a staple in many cuisines.

Capsaicin: The Chemistry of Heat

The active component in chili peppers, capsaicin, triggers a physiological response that can lead to euphoria. This reaction has led to the popularity of extreme spicy foods and contests, pushing the boundaries of culinary masochism.

12. The Garlic Divide: Odor, Superstition, and Social Boundaries

Garlic has been celebrated for its flavor and medicinal properties but also shunned for its pungent odor. Throughout history, it has been both a common seasoning and a symbol loaded with cultural meanings.

From Repellent to Remedy

In some cultures, garlic was believed to ward off evil spirits and vampires. In others, it was considered unfit for the upper classes or religious ceremonies due to its strong smell. These conflicting attitudes reflect the complex social dynamics that a simple bulb can embody.

13. Feasting/scarcity as Warfare: The Potlatch Tradition

One of the most potent means of control lies in the manipulation of food scarcity. Whether real or manufactured, food shortages have long been used to instill fear, obedience, and even xenophobia. This chapter would be incomplete without examining the role of trade embargoes, tariffs, and outright hoarding as instruments of power.

During the Irish Potato Famine, the British government capitalized on the famine to push through policies that benefited British landowners while millions starved. They created a scarcity narrative, despite abundant resources elsewhere in the Empire, to strip Irish farmers of power and reduce them to near-slavery under British rule. This was not just a food shortage; it was an orchestrated form of control.

The manipulation of food scarcity continues in modern times. With food deserts in inner cities and poverty-stricken areas, access to fresh, nutritious food is limited, keeping these communities dependent on cheap, low-quality products.

The Economics of Generosity

By hosting extravagant feasts and giving away or destroying wealth, leaders could assert their status and humiliate rivals. These practices challenge conventional notions of wealth accumulation and highlight alternative ways that societies can structure power dynamics.

In today's globalized world, many traditional food taboos have dissolved, leading to unprecedented culinary freedom. However, this abundance comes with its own set of challenges.

With everything available year-round, food can lose its seasonal and cultural significance. The absence of restrictions may lead to a lack of appreciation and a disconnect from the deeper meanings that food can convey.

Censorship and the Sanitization of Food: From Factory Farms to Supermarket Shelves

Modern food production has sanitized the process of eating to the point that many consumers have little understanding of the industry's darker side. Factory farms produce enormous quantities of meat, dairy, and eggs at the cost of animal welfare and environmental destruction. Yet in the sparkling aisles of the grocery store, this reality is masked.

The sanitization of the meat industry extends beyond visuals. Industry lobbyists have pushed for "Ag-Gag" laws in many U.S. states, which make it illegal to expose what happens behind the closed doors of factory farms. This censorship has allowed the meat industry to conceal the suffering, chemical manipulation, and health risks that are commonplace in factory farming.

The push for meat alternatives and lab-grown proteins is partly a reaction against this secrecy. However, even these innovations face pushback from lobbyists and food industry titans who see these advancements as a threat to traditional meat's profitability.

Historical Image Suggestion: Early photographs of slaughterhouses and butcheries, show the rudimentary and unsanitary conditions before modern food processing laws.

The Sugar Conspiracy: Hidden Addiction and Health Manipulation

Sugar, a staple in almost every modern diet, is one of the most insidious ingredients humanity has ever embraced. It wasn't always this way. For centuries, sugar was rare, a luxury commodity reserved for the wealthy and powerful. As sugar plantations expanded and trade routes flourished, however, sugar became increasingly affordable – and addictive.

The sugar industry has aggressively hidden the health risks associated with its products, especially in the West, where sugary beverages, snacks, and processed foods are ubiquitous. It wasn't until the late 20th century that the true dangers of sugar were widely acknowledged. Yet, even now, the sugar industry employs powerful lobbyists to ensure its product remains unrestricted.

Historically, sugar plantations were associated with slave labor and brutal working conditions, particularly in the Caribbean and South America. The demand for sugar drove a dark legacy of forced labor and inhumane treatment, legacies that many regions continue to grapple with today.

The Cultural Cleansing Through Cuisine: Colonialism's Hidden Agenda

Food has often been at the forefront of cultural imperialism. When colonizers invaded new territories, they didn't just bring armies and flags—they brought their food, imposing their diets and erasing indigenous culinary traditions. This wasn't merely about preference; it was a calculated effort to dismantle existing cultures and assert dominance.

In North America, European settlers systematically destroyed Native American food sources. They decimated bison populations, not just for meat or sport, but to starve indigenous peoples and force them into dependency. The loss of the bison was catastrophic, wiping out a cornerstone of Native American culture, economy, and spirituality.

Similarly, British colonizers in India manipulated agriculture to favor cash crops like cotton and tea over local food staples. This shift led to famines, as arable land previously used for food was now devoted to export goods. The British profited immensely, while millions of Indians suffered from hunger and poverty.

The Weaponization of Hunger: Famine as a Tool of Control

Throughout history, governments have weaponized hunger to suppress dissent and control populations. The deliberate creation or exacerbation of famines has been a ruthless strategy employed by those in power.

In the Soviet Union, Joseph Stalin orchestrated the Holodomor in the early 1930s, a man-made famine in Ukraine that killed millions. By requisitioning grain and restricting food supplies,

Stalin aimed to quash Ukrainian nationalism and resistance to collectivization. The famine was not a byproduct of mismanagement—it was a calculated act of genocide.

In China, the Great Leap Forward initiated by Mao Zedong led to the deaths of an estimated 30 million people due to starvation. While initially a misguided attempt at rapid industrialization, the government's refusal to acknowledge the famine and adjust policies turned a disaster into a prolonged tragedy.

The Opium of the Masses: Alcohol Prohibition and Social Control

Alcohol has long been a double-edged sword—used for celebration but also causing societal problems. Governments have toggled between promoting and banning alcohol to serve their interests, often under the guise of moral or public health concerns.

In the United States, the Prohibition era (1920-1933) outlawed the production and sale of alcoholic beverages. While framed as a moral crusade, Prohibition had underlying motives tied to anti-immigrant sentiment and a desire to control certain populations. Immigrant communities, particularly Irish and Italian, were stereotyped as heavy drinkers. By banning alcohol, the government targeted these groups, hoping to suppress their cultural practices and reduce their influence.

Moreover, Prohibition gave rise to organized crime, as the black market for alcohol flourished. Instead of curbing alcohol consumption, it led to increased lawlessness and corruption, demonstrating how food and drink regulations can backfire when used as tools of control.

The Hidden Hands Behind Dietary Guidelines

What we consider healthy or unhealthy is often dictated not by science but by industries with vested interests. The creation of dietary guidelines has been heavily influenced by lobbying groups, leading to recommendations that benefit corporations more than consumers.

In the mid-20th century, the sugar industry funded research to downplay the link between sugar and heart disease, shifting the blame to fats instead. This manipulation led to a low-fat craze, where fat was removed from foods and replaced with sugar to maintain flavor. The result was a surge in obesity and diabetes rates, as people unknowingly consumed more sugar under the guise of healthy eating.

Similarly, the dairy and meat industries have had significant sway over nutritional guidelines, promoting high consumption of their products despite studies linking excessive intake to health issues. The powerful marketing of these industries often overshadows independent research, shaping public perception and dietary habits.

The Dark Side of Superfoods: Quinoa and Exploitation

The rise of "superfoods" in Western markets has had unintended consequences on the countries that produce them. Quinoa, once a staple grain for indigenous communities in the Andes, became a global health trend in the early 2000s. As demand skyrocketed, prices soared, making quinoa unaffordable for the very people who relied on it as a dietary staple.

Farmers found it more profitable to export their entire crop rather than sell it locally. This shift led to nutritional deficiencies in these communities, as they turned to cheaper, less nutritious imports. The Western obsession with superfoods effectively stripped local populations of their traditional foods, highlighting the exploitative nature of global food trends.

Food Deserts and Nutritional Redlining

In many urban areas, access to fresh, healthy food is limited or nonexistent—a phenomenon known as food deserts.

Predominantly affecting low-income and minority communities, food deserts are a modern form of nutritional redlining, where systemic neglect and discriminatory policies deny certain populations access to quality food.

Convenience stores and fast-food outlets are often the only nearby options, contributing to higher rates of obesity, diabetes, and other diet-related illnesses. This lack of access isn't accidental; it's the result of urban planning decisions, economic policies, and corporate strategies that prioritize profits over people.

Efforts to introduce grocery stores and farmers' markets into these areas often face bureaucratic hurdles and a lack of funding. The persistence of food deserts reveals how food access is a social justice issue, reflecting broader patterns of inequality and discrimination.

GMOs and the Battle Over Food Sovereignty

Genetically modified organisms (GMOs) have been heralded as a solution to world hunger but have also become a flashpoint in debates over food sovereignty and corporate control. Companies like Monsanto have patented GMO seeds, requiring farmers to purchase new seeds each season instead of saving them from previous crops—a practice that has been fundamental to agriculture for millennia.

This shift has trapped farmers in a cycle of dependency, often leading to debt and loss of land. In countries like India, the introduction of GMO crops has been linked to a rise in farmer suicides, as financial pressures become overwhelming. The control of seeds—and by extension, food—by a handful of corporations poses significant threats to global food security and the autonomy of farmers.

The Silent Killer: Water as a Forbidden Resource

While not a food, water is an essential part of our diet, and access to clean water is increasingly becoming a luxury rather than a right. Corporations have privatized water sources around the world, bottling and selling what was once freely available. In some regions, communities are denied access to their water supplies, which are diverted for commercial use.

In places like Flint, Michigan, and parts of South Africa, contaminated water has led to health crises. These situations are often the result of neglect, corruption, or profit-driven policies that prioritize industry over people. The commodification of water raises ethical questions about basic human rights and highlights the growing inequality in resource distribution.

The Diet of Incarceration: Food as Punishment

In prisons and detention centers, food is often used as a tool for punishment and control. Meals are nutritionally inadequate, unappetizing, and sometimes intentionally so. The infamous "Nutraloaf," a concoction served in some U.S. prisons, is a prime example—a bland, loaf-like substance given to inmates as disciplinary action.

This misuse of food goes beyond neglect; it's a deliberate strategy to dehumanize and exert power over incarcerated individuals. Such practices raise concerns about human rights and the ethical treatment of prisoners, highlighting the broader issues within the criminal justice system.

The Globalization of Fast Food: Cultural Erosion and Health Impacts

The spread of Western fast-food chains across the globe has had profound effects on local cuisines, health, and economies. Traditional diets rich in vegetables, grains, and lean proteins are being replaced with high-fat, high-sugar, and highly processed foods. This shift has led to rising obesity rates and related health issues in countries previously unaffected by such epidemics.

Moreover, the dominance of multinational corporations in the food industry undermines local businesses and food traditions. As global brands become symbols of modernity and status, they erode cultural identities tied to indigenous foods and practices.

Rediscovering Meaning in What We Eat

The forbidden history of food reveals that our choices at the table are about more than personal preference; they are expressions of identity, morality, and power. As we navigate a world where fewer foods are off-limits, it becomes crucial to understand the historical contexts that have shaped our culinary landscapes.

By acknowledging the complex tapestry of beliefs and practices surrounding food, we can make more informed choices that respect both our heritage and our evolving values. Perhaps in doing so, we can restore some of the lost meaning to one of the most fundamental aspects of human life.

Chapter 22: The Forbidden History of Surgical Instruments/Medicine

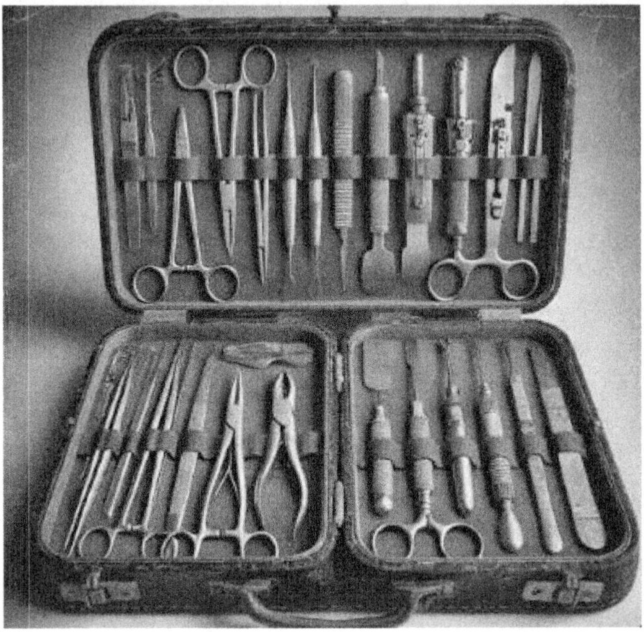

Medicine and surgery have long been heralded as the pinnacles of human ingenuity and compassion. Yet, beneath the surface of celebrated breakthroughs lies a hidden history—a chronicle of tools and practices that modern medicine prefers to forget. This chapter delves into the shadowy evolution of surgical instruments and medical procedures, exposing the untold stories and forbidden knowledge that shaped today's healthcare landscape.

Unveiling The Surgeon's Tools

When we think of surgery, images of sterile environments and precise instruments come to mind. However, the journey to modern surgical practice is paved with rudimentary tools and daring innovations that pushed the boundaries of medical ethics and human endurance.

In the late 19th century, surgeons like Gustav Weber amassed a vast array of instruments that would baffle even the most seasoned practitioners today. Weber's collection wasn't limited to a specific specialty; it spanned ophthalmic tools, laryngeal devices, amputation sets, and experimental equipment like the electro-cautery apparatus.

Unlike the specialized surgeons of today, Weber practiced at a time when a surgeon was expected to handle any case that came through the door. From reconstructive surgeries to amputations, the breadth of his practice was as expansive as his instrument collection.

International Influences and Personal Preferences

Weber's instruments were sourced globally, reflecting a cosmopolitan approach uncommon for his time. He favored German and Austrian manufacturers like Kramer of Bonn and Josef Leiter of Vienna over local American makers.

Weber's preference wasn't merely about quality; it was personal. His ties to Europe maintained through frequent trips and subscriptions to European medical journals, influenced his choices. He even sent his son to study in Bonn, reinforcing the deep-rooted connections that guided his professional decisions.

The late 19th century saw the medical community grappling with the germ theory of disease. While some embraced new antiseptic methods, others were hesitant.

Tradition vs. Innovation

Weber's instrument collection revealed a paradox. Despite his awareness of germ theory and antiseptic practices, many of his tools were made from traditional materials like ivory and ebony—materials that couldn't withstand sterilization processes.

Weber wasn't entirely resistant to change. He adopted antiseptic procedures like carbolic acid sprays and even encouraged younger surgeons to use all-metal instruments. Yet, he continued to use his trusted tools, balancing innovation with familiarity.

Diagnostic Instruments: The New Eyes and Ears

The 19th century introduced diagnostic tools that revolutionized how physicians examined patients, shifting from subjective assessments to objective measurements.

1. **The Ophthalmoscope: Peering into the Soul**

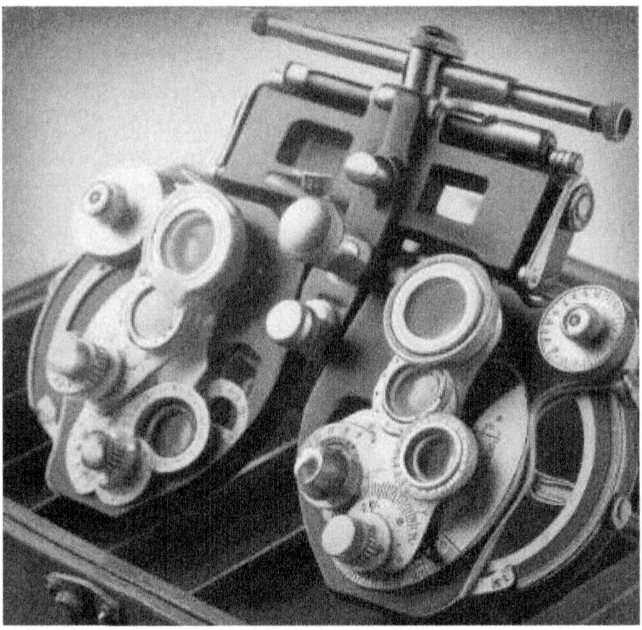

Invented by Hermann von Helmholtz around 1850, the ophthalmoscope allowed doctors to look inside the eye, revealing not just ocular conditions but systemic diseases like diabetes and hypertension.

While one might assume such instruments led to specialization, they were used by general practitioners as well. The ability to diagnose a range of conditions made the ophthalmoscope an invaluable tool in a surgeon's kit.

2. **The Otoscope and Thermoscope: Expanding Sensory Boundaries**

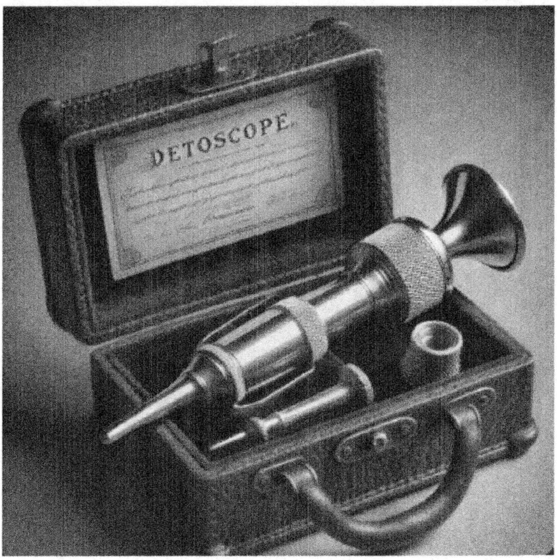

Devices like the otoscope and thermoscope emerged, enabling doctors to examine the ear and measure body temperature with newfound accuracy.

These instruments marked a shift towards precision medicine. The thermoscope, for instance, could detect localized infections by measuring slight variations in body temperature—a significant advancement from the rudimentary assessments of the past.

3. The Rise and Fall of the Sphygmograph and Sphygmomanometer

Measuring the Pulse and Pressure

The sphygmograph and sphygmomanometer were early attempts to quantify the pulse and blood pressure, offering visual and numerical data that promised to refine diagnoses.

Despite their innovative designs, these instruments were plagued by inconsistencies and technical difficulties. Variations between devices made standardization impossible, limiting their clinical utility.

While flawed, these devices laid the groundwork for future innovations in cardiovascular diagnostics, highlighting the relentless pursuit of medical advancement despite setbacks.

4. The Microscope: Unlocking Invisible Worlds

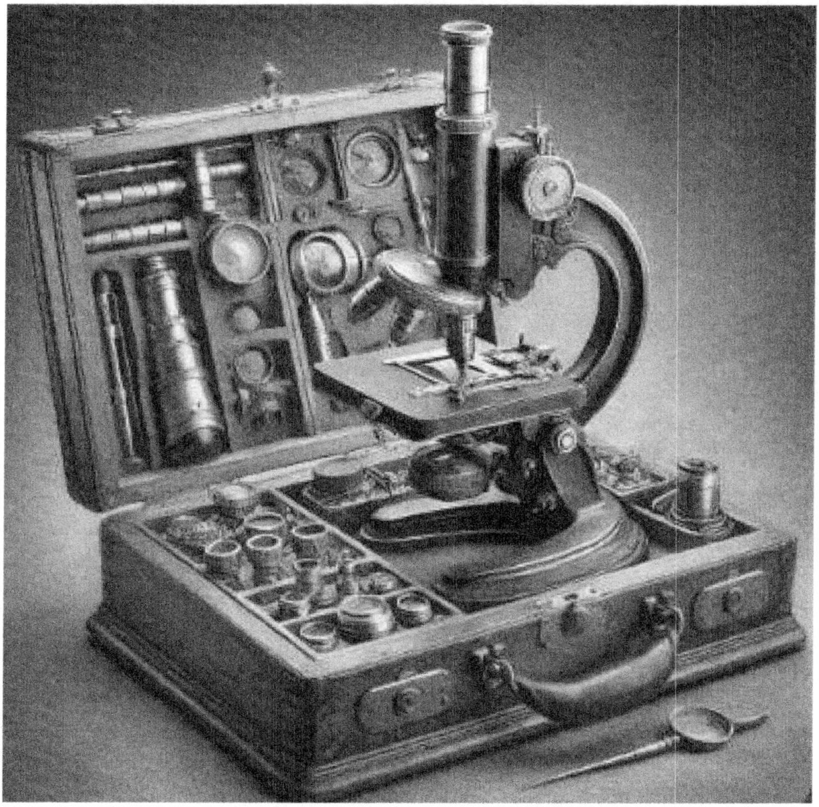

The microscope's journey into medical practice was transformative, allowing for the study of tissues and pathogens at the cellular level.

Early microscopes were expensive and complex, often limited to well-funded institutions and affluent practitioners like Weber.

5. **Post-Mortem Practices: Dissecting Death**

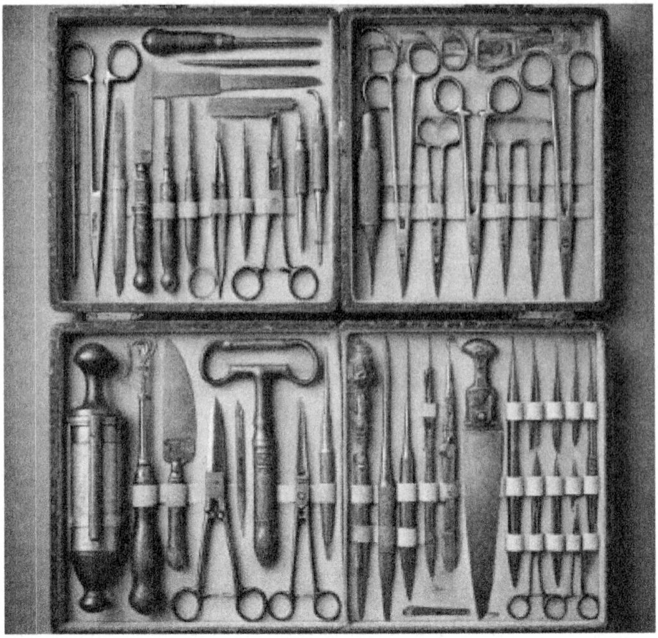

Autopsies were essential for medical education and understanding disease, but they were shrouded in controversy and ethical dilemmas.

Weber's post-mortem sets included specialized instruments like enterotomes for opening intestines and chisels for removing the skull cap.

Dissection often skirted legal boundaries, with bodies sometimes acquired through dubious means. The demand for cadavers led to a macabre underworld that modern medicine prefers to ignore.

6. **The Brutality of Amputation and Military Medicine**

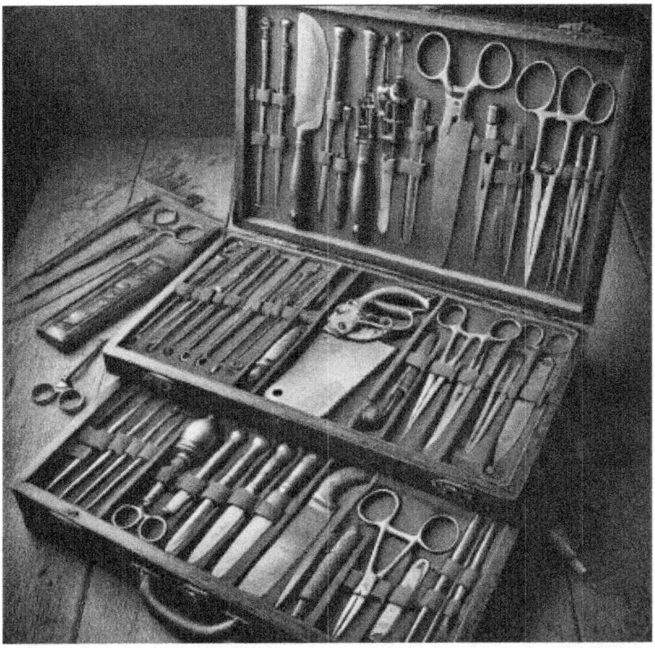

War has always been a catalyst for medical advancements, albeit born from necessity rather than compassion.

During the Civil War, surgeons like Weber faced unprecedented challenges, performing amputations at a staggering rate with limited resources.

The design of surgical kits evolved to meet the demands of war, becoming more portable and versatile. These sets often included tools for quick amputations, reflecting the grim realities of battlefield medicine.

7. The Nelaton Probe: Seeking Bullets in Flesh

Developed to locate bullets lodged deep within the body, the Nelaton probe was a simple yet ingenious instrument that saved countless lives.

8. Minor Surgery: The Delicate Dance

Not all surgical procedures were grand operations; many were minor yet required precision and specialized tools.

Pocket Cases and Personal Kits

Physicians carried small cases filled with scalpels, forceps, and needles, ready to perform minor surgeries at a moment's notice.

These minor surgeries, though less dramatic, were crucial in treating infections, removing small tumors, and alleviating immediate pain, showcasing the surgeon's versatility.

9. The Osteotome: A Mechanical Marvel

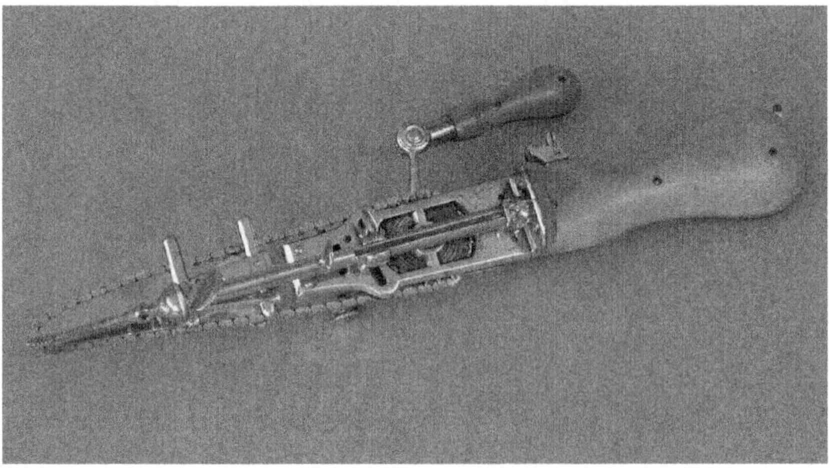

Photo taken at Orthopädische Universitätsklinik Frankfurt (M)

Bernhard Heine's osteotome revolutionized bone surgery by introducing a device that allowed for precise cuts with minimal damage.

The osteotome was essentially a chainsaw for bones, using a crank to drive a chain of sharp links around a guiding frame.

Despite its innovation, the osteotome was expensive and complicated, limiting its widespread adoption. It stands as a testament to the lengths surgeons would go to improve patient outcomes.

10. Trephining: Drilling into the Mind

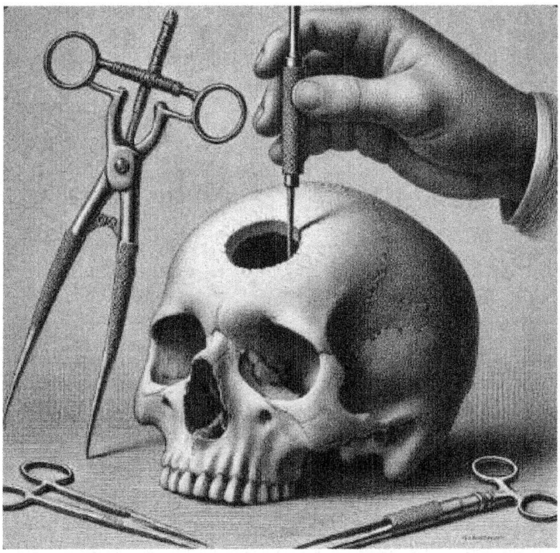

An ancient practice, trephining involved removing sections of the skull to treat head injuries or relieve pressure.

Used since prehistoric times, trephining in the 19th century still carried significant risks, with high mortality rates due to infection and lack of anesthesia.

Weber's trephining set included devices that changed little over centuries, highlighting the persistence of certain medical practices despite advancements elsewhere.

11. Cleft Palate Surgery: Merging Art and Science

Correcting cleft palates required intricate procedures and specialized instruments, reflecting a blend of surgical skills and creative problem-solving.

Bernhard von Langenbeck developed a method to repair hard palate clefts by manipulating the periosteum and utilizing innovative suturing techniques.

These surgeries not only improved physical function but also had profound social and psychological impacts on patients, underscoring the holistic role of surgical intervention.

12. Tracheostomy and Laryngeal Instruments: Opening Airways

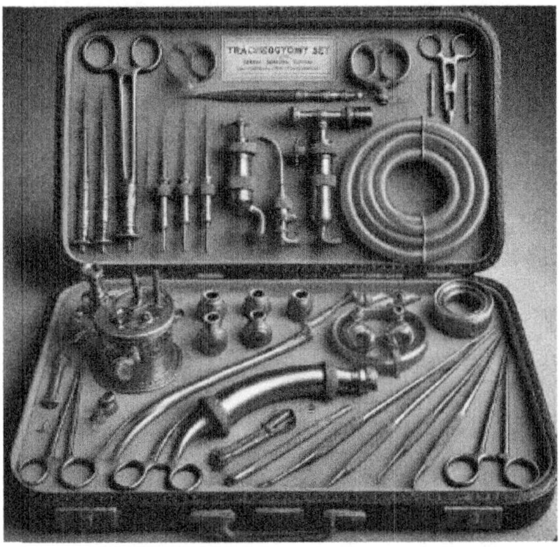

Tracheostomy, the act of creating an opening in the trachea to facilitate breathing, evolved significantly during Weber's time.

Diseases like diphtheria necessitated emergency procedures to prevent suffocation, leading to the development of specialized tracheostomy tubes and dilators.

While life-saving, tracheostomies carried high risks of infection and mortality. Surgeons continually refined their techniques and tools to improve outcomes.

13. Galvano-Cautery: Harnessing Electricity

The application of electricity in surgery opened new frontiers, with devices like the galvano-cautery enabling precise tissue removal with reduced bleeding.

Albrecht Middeldorpf pioneered the use of heated platinum wires powered by galvanic batteries to cauterize tissues.

Early devices were cumbersome and unreliable, hindered by inconsistent power sources and fragile components. Yet, they represented a significant leap towards modern electro-surgical techniques.

14. The Aspirator: Drawing Out Disease

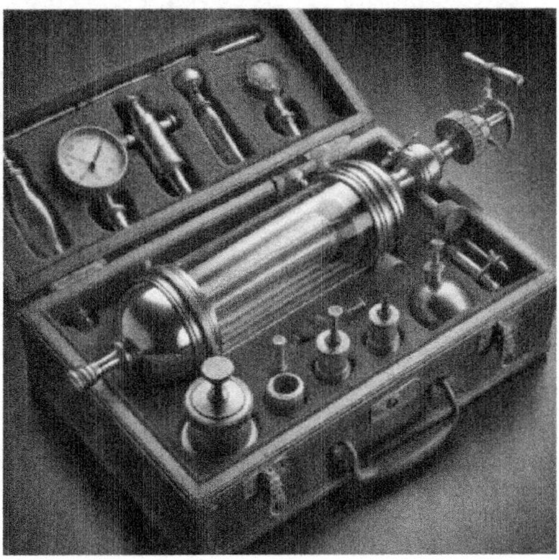

The development of the aspirator allowed surgeons to remove fluids from body cavities with minimal invasion, a crucial advancement in treating conditions like pleural effusions.

From simple syringes to complex vacuum devices, aspirators became more efficient and safer over time.

The aspirator reduced the risks associated with earlier methods like trocars, which often led to infections due to exposure to air and contaminants.

15. The Stomach Pump: A Double-Edged Sword

Initially designed to treat poisoning, the stomach pump found broader applications in diagnosing and treating gastric diseases.

Adolf Kussmaul refined the stomach pump, making it a diagnostic tool to extract and analyze stomach contents.

While effective, the stomach pump could be traumatic for patients, sometimes causing more harm than good. Its use highlighted the ethical considerations of invasive diagnostics.

16. Lithotomy and Lithotrity: Battling Bladder Stones

The removal of bladder stones was a common yet risky procedure, with techniques evolving from surgical removal to less invasive methods.

Lithotomy involved making incisions to extract stones, while lithotrity introduced instruments to crush stones internally.

Henry Bigelow's innovation allowed for complete stone removal in a single session, reducing patient discomfort and the risk of complications.

17. Ophthalmic Surgery: Delicate Interventions

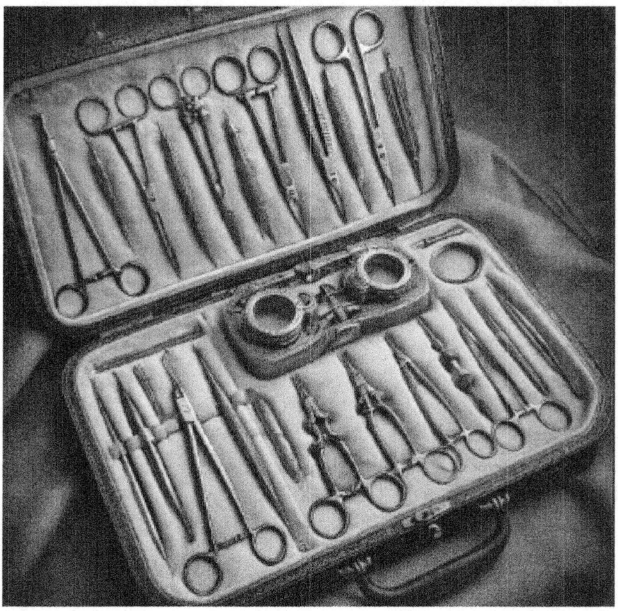

Eye surgery requires precision and finesse, with instruments specially designed for intricate procedures.

Weber's collection included tools for cataract removal, iridectomy, and treating strabismus, reflecting the complexity of ophthalmic surgery.

Surgeons emphasized lightweight instruments to enhance control and reduce fatigue, a principle that remains relevant today.

18. Hypodermic Syringes: Revolutionizing Medication Delivery

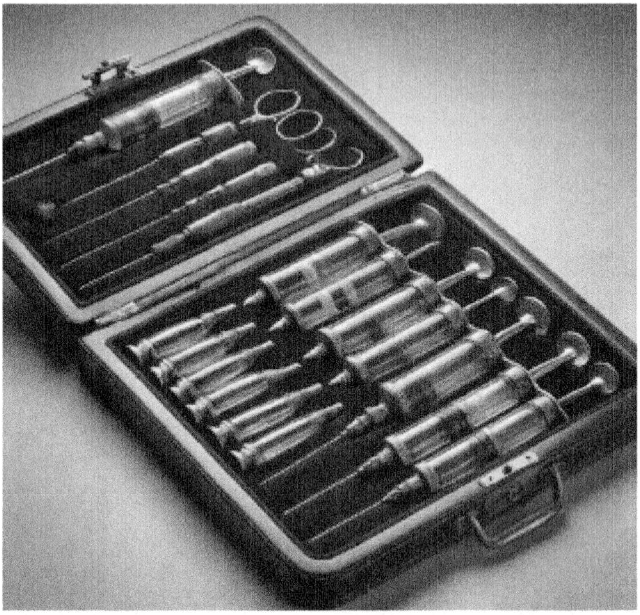

The advent of hypodermic syringes transformed medical treatment, allowing for direct administration of drugs into the bloodstream.

Initial designs were prone to leaks and breakage, but improvements led to reliable syringes that became staples in medical practice.

Hypodermic administration opened new avenues for pain management and treatment of various conditions, marking a significant shift in pharmacology.

19. Transfusion Apparatus: The Lifeblood of Survival

Blood transfusion devices attempted to combat hemorrhage, particularly in obstetrics, despite a limited understanding of blood compatibility.

The use of direct transfusion from donor to recipient with basic tubing and a squeeze bulb exemplified the ingenuity of the time.

Without knowledge of blood types, transfusions were risky endeavors. The high failure rate underscored the gap between technological capability and scientific understanding.

20. Gynecological and Obstetrical Instruments: Breaking Taboos

The development of instruments for women's health challenged societal norms and pushed the boundaries of medical ethics.

Despite cultural resistance, the speculum became an essential tool for diagnosing and treating gynecological conditions.

The speculum symbolized both the advancement of women's healthcare and the intrusion of male-dominated medicine into female spaces, reflecting the complexities of progress.

The evolution of surgical instruments and medical practices is a story of the relentless pursuit of knowledge intertwined with ethical quandaries and human suffering. The forbidden history of these tools reveals the cost of progress and the shadows that linger behind the bright lights of modern medicine.

The instruments may have evolved, but the responsibility to wield them with wisdom and compassion remains a constant mandate for all in the medical field.

Part V: The Veiled Mechanisms of Influence

This section unravels the hidden narratives that mainstream history often overlooks or deliberately suppresses, providing a comprehensive exploration of how power intertwines with religion, geological transformations, scientific fraud, cultural advancements, and the puzzling history of Africa's hominid evolution.

Chapter 23: Persecuted Faith: The Untold Story of Muslims and Moriscos in Colonial Spanish America

This chapter exposes the deeply suppressed history of Muslims and Moriscos in the Spanish New World colonies between 1512 and 1659. Despite the Spanish Crown's strict prohibition against their migration, approximately 48 individuals either practiced Islam or were accused of Morisco heritage. These individuals, including notable figures like Diego Romero, navigated a hostile environment marked by the relentless persecution of the Spanish Inquisition. The chapter details how colonial authorities used cultural practices as pretexts for accusations, forcing forced conversions and cultural assimilation to maintain religious and cultural homogeneity. Slavery provided a loophole for some Moriscos, yet they remained vulnerable to suspicion and repression, highlighting the systemic efforts to erase their identities and heritage.

Chapter 24: The Forbidden History of the Earth's Shifting Crust

Natural disasters and geological transformations have always played pivotal roles in shaping human history. Yet, the intricate relationship between geological events and societal upheavals is often underrepresented in mainstream historical accounts. This chapter examines how earthquakes, volcanic eruptions, and tectonic shifts have influenced the rise and fall of civilizations. We delve into instances where natural catastrophes were either exploited by ruling powers to consolidate control or suppressed to prevent mass panic and maintain stability. Furthermore, the chapter investigates how ancient societies interpreted and mythologized geological phenomena, intertwining them with religious and cultural beliefs to reinforce societal hierarchies and control narratives.

Chapter 25: Piltdown's Find – A Forgery Unveiled

The Piltdown Man scandal remains one of the most infamous scientific frauds in history. Presented as the missing link between apes and humans, this supposed fossil discovery captivated the scientific community and the public alike. This chapter meticulously deconstructs the Piltdown forgery, exploring the motivations behind the deception, the methods used to fabricate evidence, and the profound impact it had on the field of anthropology. We analyze how the scandal influenced scientific thought, delayed genuine discoveries in human evolution, and highlighted the vulnerabilities within the scientific community to bias and fraud. The chapter also draws parallels to modern scientific controversies, emphasizing the enduring lessons learned from the Piltdown debacle.

Chapter 26: The Forbidden History of Our Advanced Culture

Modern advancements in technology, science, and culture often come with hidden costs and ethical dilemmas that are glossed over in popular narratives. This chapter scrutinizes the underbelly of cultural and technological progress, revealing how innovations intended to elevate humanity have sometimes led to societal fragmentation, loss of privacy, and ethical compromises. From the rise of surveillance states enabled by technological advancements to the cultural homogenization driven by globalization, we uncover the unintended consequences of progress. Additionally, the chapter explores how media and popular culture have been manipulated to shape public opinion, suppress dissenting voices, and perpetuate consumerism, thereby maintaining existing power structures and economic interests.

Chapter 27: Ape-Like Men and the Forbidden History of Africa

The study of human evolution has been marred by biases and controversies, particularly concerning the representation of African hominids. This chapter delves into the often-suppressed narratives of Africa's pivotal role in human evolution, challenging Eurocentric perspectives that have historically marginalized African contributions. We investigate how colonialism and racism influenced early anthropological studies, leading to the misrepresentation and underestimation of African hominid fossils. The chapter also explores recent breakthroughs in paleoanthropology that have redefined our understanding of human origins, highlighting the rich and diverse evolutionary history rooted in the African continent. By shedding light on these forbidden histories, we aim to rectify historical inaccuracies and acknowledge Africa's undeniable significance in the story of humanity.

Part V of *Forbidden History: History That Is Not Allowed Will Blow Your Mind* serves as a critical examination of the concealed forces that have shaped human civilization. By exposing the hidden mechanisms of power within religion, geological transformations, scientific fraud, cultural advancements, and evolutionary studies, we gain a deeper understanding of the complexities and often dark undercurrents that drive historical change. This exploration not only challenges conventional narratives but also underscores the importance of scrutinizing the stories we accept as truth.

Chapter 23: Persecuted Faith: The Untold Story of Muslims and Moriscos in Colonial Spanish America

Religion has always been a cornerstone of societal identity, shaping cultures, laws, and interpersonal relationships. However, beneath the surface of mainstream historical narratives lies a tumultuous and often suppressed history of religious intolerance and persecution. Among the most overlooked and forbidden chapters in this saga is the story of Muslims and Moriscos in the Spanish New World colonies between 1512 and 1659. This chapter delves into the clandestine lives of these individuals, the brutal measures taken against them, and the profound impact their presence had on the formation of Spanish colonial identity.

The Shadows of Exclusion: Muslims and Moriscos in Colonial America

In the early 16th century, as Spain embarked on its ambitious colonization of the Americas, a dark undercurrent of religious intolerance simmered beneath the veneer of conquest and conversion. The Spanish Crown, driven by a zealous commitment to Catholicism, officially prohibited the entry of Muslims and Moriscos into its expanding empire. This policy was not merely a religious decree but a strategic move to maintain cultural and religious homogeneity within the colonies. The suppression of Muslim and Morisco presence was integral to the broader objective of consolidating Spanish power and ensuring the unchallenged spread of Catholicism in the New World.

Uncovering the Hidden Figures: Documented Muslims and Moriscos

The scarcity of records and the deliberate suppression of information make it challenging to trace the lives of Muslims and Moriscos in the Spanish New World. However, through meticulous research and the examination of fragmented archival materials, Karoline Cook identifies approximately 48 documented individuals accused of being Muslims or Moriscos between 1512 and 1659. These individuals, though few, played a significant role in the cultural and social dynamics of the colonies.

One of the most compelling case studies is that of Diego Romero, an allegedly escaped Morisco slave who became a prominent figure in the early Spanish colonial history of Colombia and Venezuela. Romero arrived in the Americas as a free man and participated actively in Gonzalo Jiménez de Quesada's conquests. His heroism and subsequent wealth as an encomendero lord highlight the complex interplay between identity, power, and survival in the colonial context. Despite his achievements, Romero was later imprisoned on suspicions of his Morisco origins, illustrating the persistent threat of persecution that shadowed Muslim and Morisco individuals.

The Inquisition's Grim Grip: Trials and Tribulations

The Spanish Inquisition was the primary instrument of religious persecution, targeting not only heretics but also those suspected of harboring Muslim or Morisco affiliations. In Lima, for example, internal conflicts within the Inquisition tribunal revealed that even powerful officials' households were rife with Moriscos. These tribunals often relied on dubious evidence and coerced testimonies, making accusations of Morisco's identity a tool for political and social maneuvering.

In many instances, individuals were accused based on cultural practices rather than concrete evidence of their faith. Activities deemed "Morisco-like," such as love magic or healing arts, became grounds for suspicion and punishment. This broad definition of Morisco extended beyond actual converts, encompassing "Old Christian" settlers and even Indigenous peoples who engaged in or were aware of such practices. The transatlantic transfer of cultures facilitated by these interactions further blurred the lines between different religious and cultural identities, complicating the Inquisition's mission of maintaining religious purity.

Forced Assimilation and Cultural Erasure

The Spanish Crown's policies were not solely aimed at persecution but also forced assimilation. Muslims and Moriscos were compelled to abandon their cultural and religious practices, often under the threat of severe punishment. Conversion to Christianity was mandatory, and those who resisted faced excommunication, imprisonment, or even execution. This forced assimilation was designed to eradicate Islamic influences and reinforce Catholic orthodoxy, ensuring that the colonial society remained aligned with Spanish religious and cultural norms.

The impact of these policies was profound. Muslim and Morisco individuals were stripped of their identities, forced to adopt new names, and prohibited from practicing their faith openly. The suppression of Islamic culture in the colonies was a deliberate attempt to erase any remnants of Muslim heritage, creating a homogeneous religious landscape that supported Spanish colonial objectives.

The Role of Slavery: Moriscos in Bondage

While the Spanish Crown officially prohibited Muslim and Morisco migration, exceptions were made for slaves owned by powerful settlers. Many Moriscos arrived in the Americas in bondage, where their status as slaves offered a veneer of protection against immediate persecution. However, their enslaved status did not shield them from the broader anti-Morisco sentiment and the constant threat of accusation and punishment.

Moriscos in slavery were often subjected to harsh conditions and forced to assimilate into the dominant Christian culture. Despite their difficult circumstances, some managed to maintain aspects of their Islamic heritage, subtly incorporating their faith and cultural practices into their daily lives. These acts of resistance, though small, were significant in preserving a sense of identity and community among the enslaved Moriscos.

The Unrelenting Pursuit of Identity: Accusations and Reputations

Accusations of Morisco's identity were not limited to official tribunals. Social ostracism and reputational damage were also common tactics used to marginalize and control Muslim and Morisco individuals. Community members and neighbors often played a role in identifying and reporting suspected Moriscos, driven by fear, prejudice, or personal vendettas. This pervasive suspicion created an environment of constant vigilance and insecurity for those who were or were perceived to be Moriscos.

In some cases, individuals went to great lengths to conceal their true identities, adopting Christian names, altering their appearances, and suppressing any outward signs of their Islamic heritage. Despite these efforts, the deeply ingrained prejudices and systemic mechanisms of control ensured that the threat of discovery and punishment remained ever-present.

Cultural Syncretism: The Hidden Legacy of Moriscos

Despite the intense persecution and efforts at forced assimilation, the Morisco presence left a lasting, albeit hidden, legacy in the Spanish New World colonies. Cultural syncretism, the blending of different cultural and religious traditions, became a survival mechanism for Moriscos, allowing them to retain aspects of their heritage while outwardly conforming to Christian norms.

This blending can be seen in various aspects of colonial life, from language and cuisine to religious practices and architectural styles. Morisco's influence subtly permeated the cultural fabric of the colonies, contributing to the rich and diverse heritage of Latin America. However, the extent of this influence often went unrecognized or was deliberately obscured by dominant narratives that sought to erase the presence of Muslims and Moriscos.

The Persistence of Morisco Identity: A Testament to Resilience

The resilience of Morisco individuals in the face of relentless persecution is a testament to their enduring spirit and determination to preserve their identity. Despite the harsh conditions and constant threats, many Moriscos managed to maintain their cultural and religious practices in secret, passing them down through generations.

This persistence was not just a personal struggle but a collective effort to sustain a community and resist cultural erasure. The clandestine continuation of Islamic traditions within the colonies highlights the deep-rooted connections and the powerful drive to maintain one's heritage against overwhelming odds.

The history of Muslims and Moriscos in the Spanish New World colonies is a powerful reminder of how religion can be weaponized to enforce conformity, suppress diversity, and maintain control. The suppression of Morisco's identity was not merely a series of isolated incidents but a concerted effort to mold colonial society in the image of the Spanish Crown's religious and cultural ideals.

By uncovering this forbidden history, we gain a deeper understanding of the complexities and contradictions that shaped the Spanish Empire in the Americas. It challenges the sanitized narratives of conquest and conversion, revealing the darker underpinnings of religious intolerance and cultural suppression that have long been overlooked or deliberately hidden.

Chapter 24: The Forbidden History of the Earth's Shifting Crust

In the relentless pursuit of uncovering the secrets of lost civilizations, one theory has been systematically sidelined by mainstream science: Earth's crust displacement. This radical concept challenges the very foundation of our understanding of geology and ancient history, suggesting that entire continents have shifted their positions over relatively short geological periods. If proven true, it would revolutionize our comprehension of human history, archaeology, and the natural world. Yet, this theory remains buried in the shadows of academic orthodoxy, deemed heretical by many experts. This chapter delves into the forbidden history of Earth's shifting crust, exposing the suppression of groundbreaking ideas and the potential revelations that await beneath the ice.

The Paradigm-Shifting Theory of Crustal Displacement

The conventional model of plate tectonics, which describes the movement of large plates composing the Earth's surface, has been the cornerstone of geological science for decades. However, in the mid-20th century, an alternative theory emerged, proposing that the Earth's entire outer shell can shift dramatically over its inner layers. Pioneered by Dr. Charles Hapgood, this theory of Earth crust displacement posits that such shifts can occur relatively quickly, geologically speaking, leading to catastrophic climatic and geographical changes.

Hapgood's theory gained momentum through his collaboration with none other than Albert Einstein, lending it an unexpected credibility. Their correspondence revealed a mutual interest in challenging the status quo and exploring uncharted scientific territories. Hapgood argued that periodic shifts of the Earth's crust could account for various geological anomalies and historical mysteries, including the enigmatic disappearance of civilizations like Atlantis.

Rand and Rose Flem-Ath: Guardians of a Hidden Legacy

Canadian researchers Rand and Rose Flem-Ath have been instrumental in resurrecting and expanding upon Hapgood's ideas. Their seminal work, *When the Sky Fell: In Search of Atlantis*, synthesizes Hapgood's theory with their own archaeological and geological findings. The Flem-Aths propose that the legendary city of Atlantis was not a mythological construct but a real, advanced civilization that thrived on what is now Antarctica before being obliterated by a sudden crustal shift.

Their research challenges the conventional locations proposed for Atlantis, such as the North Atlantic and the Aegean Sea, by shifting the focus to the frozen continent of Antarctica. This audacious claim aligns with the shifting perspectives of other researchers like John Anthony West and Graham Hancock, who have long advocated for revisiting ancient myths and aligning them with geological evidence.

Decoding Ancient Maps: Athenasius Kircher and Piri Reis

A critical element supporting the theory of crustal displacement is the analysis of ancient maps that seem to prefigure modern geographical features with startling accuracy. Two such maps have become central to this argument: the 1665 map by Jesuit scholar Athenasius Kircher and the 1513 Piri Reis map.

Kircher's map, though created centuries after Plato's account of Atlantis, positions the legendary continent in the North Atlantic and intriguingly orients it north at the bottom. This inversion suggests an awareness of landmass dynamics that could only be explained by a shifting crust. Similarly, the Piri Reis map, which includes detailed depictions of coastlines now submerged under ice, implies advanced surveying knowledge far beyond what was believed possible at the time.

Rand Flem-Ath posits that these maps are not mere cartographic curiosities but are instead remnants of an advanced Atlantean survey conducted before the last crustal displacement. By aligning these ancient representations with modern coordinates, the Flem-Aths argue that the historical accounts of Atlantis are not fabrications but echoes of a once-glorious civilization disrupted by geological upheaval.

Sacred Latitudes: The Geodetic Blueprint of Atlantis

One of the most compelling pieces of evidence presented by Rand and Rose Flem-Ath is the concept of "sacred latitudes." These are specific geographical lines that ancient civilizations aligned their most significant sites with, corresponding to the Earth's former positions before the crustal displacement. The Flem-Aths identified recurring sacred latitudes at 0°, 12°, 15°, 30°, and 45°—each of which divides the Earth's geography into precise, meaningful segments.

For instance, the Great Pyramid of Giza, currently located at 30° north, was situated at 15° north before the displacement. Similarly, Lhasa, now at approximately 30° north, was once positioned near the equator. These precise shifts suggest that ancient architects had an intricate understanding of the Earth's geodesy, likely a legacy of Atlantean knowledge that predates our current scientific advancements.

Ancient Sites as Geodesic Markers

The alignment of ancient sites extends beyond Egypt and Tibet. Sites like Teotihuacan in Mexico, Ur and Uruk in Mesopotamia, and Jerusalem's Wailing Wall all exhibit orientations that align with these sacred latitudes. These alignments are too consistent to be mere coincidences, indicating a deliberate geodesic mapping system that was likely disrupted by the crustal displacement.

In Teotihuacan, the Street of the Dead is misaligned by 15.5°, directly pointing towards the Pleiades constellation—an alignment that resonates with Atlantean celestial navigation.

Similarly, the Great Pyramid of Giza's precise orientation toward ancient polar positions suggests an intentional, knowledge-driven design rather than random placement.

The Collision of Myth and Science

The integration of mythological narratives with geological theories presents a formidable challenge to traditional academia. Plato's accounts of Atlantis, often dismissed as allegorical, gain new relevance when considered alongside geological evidence of crustal displacement. The Flem-Aths argue that these myths are encoded historical records, preserving the memory of a cataclysmic event that reshaped the Earth and erased a civilization from history.

This intersection of myth and science forces a reevaluation of ancient texts. Plato's detailed descriptions of Atlantis's grandeur, technological prowess, and sudden demise mirror the proposed effects of a rapid crustal shift. The legends of Atlantis, therefore, may be more than stories—they could be the last remnants of a real civilization grappling with environmental catastrophe.

Geological Catastrophes and Civilizational Collapse

The theory of crustal displacement provides a plausible explanation for the rapid decline of advanced civilizations. If entire continents can shift, relocating significant landmasses from temperate to polar regions, the resulting environmental changes would be devastating. Ice caps could encroach upon habitable areas, sea levels could rise dramatically, and climate zones could become inhospitable almost overnight.

The Flem-Aths correlate this with the disappearance of Atlantis, suggesting that the civilization was obliterated by such a displacement. The destruction would have been so swift and comprehensive that it left no trace in the geological record beyond what has been obscured by ice and sediment.

Reconstructing the Lost World: Technological and Archaeological Implications

If the Earth's crust can shift in the manner proposed, it necessitates a complete overhaul of our archaeological and geological methodologies. Traditional excavations would need to account for displaced landmasses, and satellite imagery would become indispensable in identifying anomalies that suggest past shifts.

Moreover, the possibility of finding preserved artifacts under ice caps opens new avenues for exploration. These frozen relics could offer unprecedented insights into Atlantean technology, culture, and daily life, providing tangible evidence to support the theory of a lost advanced civilization.

The Resistance of Mainstream Science

Despite the compelling nature of crustal displacement theory, it faces staunch opposition from the scientific community. Established geologists and tectonics experts dismiss the notion as pseudoscience, arguing that plate tectonics sufficiently explains continental movement over millions of years without necessitating sudden, large-scale shifts.

The resistance is partly due to the lack of direct evidence and the dramatic paradigm shift required to accept crustal displacement. Furthermore, the theory undermines the credibility of long-established geological principles, making it a contentious topic within academic circles.

The Potential Breakthrough: Modern Technology as a Catalyst

Advancements in technology, particularly satellite imaging and seismic monitoring, hold the key to unlocking the mysteries of crustal displacement. High-resolution satellite images can detect subtle geological anomalies that may indicate past shifts, while comprehensive seismic surveys can provide data on the Earth's subsurface movements.

Rand and Rose Flem-Ath advocate for targeted exploration of Antarctica, arguing that focused research could yield definitive evidence of Atlantis. The presence of advanced ancient civilizations beneath the ice is a tantalizing possibility that could reshape our understanding of human history and the Earth's geological processes.

The forbidden history of Earth's shifting crust is not merely an academic curiosity—it is a potential revelation that could alter our perception of the past and our place in the world. The suppression of such theories by mainstream science underscores a broader issue of intellectual stagnation, where groundbreaking ideas are dismissed without thorough examination.

As we stand on the brink of unprecedented technological advancements, the time is ripe to revisit and rigorously test the theory of crustal displacement. The implications of confirming such a shift are profound, extending beyond geology into the realms of archaeology, history, and even mythology. The lost continent of Atlantis, once relegated to the annals of legend, may hold the key to unlocking our true heritage and understanding the forces that have shaped our planet.

Chapter 25: Piltdown Man—Unveiling the Greatest Scientific Forgery

The early 20th century was a time of fervent anticipation in the scientific community. The search for the elusive "missing link" between apes and humans had intensified following the discovery of Homo erectus fossils in Java by Eugene Dubois in the 1890s. In this charged atmosphere, a sensational find emerged from the English countryside that promised to fill a crucial gap in human evolution: the Piltdown Man. Heralded as Eoanthropus dawsoni, or "Dawson's Dawn Man," this discovery captivated the world—only to be exposed decades later as one of the most elaborate and impactful hoaxes in scientific history.

This chapter delves deep into the enigmatic tale of the Piltdown Man, unraveling the intricate web of ambition, deception, and scientific fervor that allowed a forgery to persist unquestioned for over 40 years. We will explore how this incident not only misled the scientific community but also offers a cautionary tale about the vulnerabilities inherent in the pursuit of knowledge.

The Discovery That Shook the World

In 1908, Charles Dawson, a solicitor and amateur archaeologist with a penchant for fossil hunting, made a discovery that would soon capture global attention. Near the village of Piltdown in Sussex, England, he unearthed fragments of a skull and jawbone that appeared to possess both human and ape-like features. Over the next few years, Dawson, often accompanied by Arthur Smith Woodward, the esteemed Keeper of Geology at the British Museum, continued excavations at the site. They uncovered more fragments, including a section of jawbone with two molar teeth, flint tools, and fossilized animal remains.

On December 18, 1912, Dawson and Woodward announced their findings to the Geological Society of London. The Piltdown Man was hailed as the oldest known human ancestor, estimated to be over 500,000 years old. Its unique combination of a human-like cranium and an ape-like jaw seemed to provide the long-sought transitional fossil—a true "missing link."

The Scientific Enthusiasm and Acceptance

The Piltdown Man fit neatly into the expectations of many scientists of the time. It provided a Eurocentric origin of humanity, bolstering the belief that England could be the cradle of mankind. The discovery was widely accepted by prominent scientists and featured in textbooks and evolutionary charts. It influenced theories on human evolution, suggesting that the development of a large brain preceded other human characteristics.

Notably, Sir Arthur Keith, a leading anatomist, supported the Piltdown findings, incorporating them into his model of human evolution. The fossils were seen as validation of the idea that brain enlargement was the driving force in human development.

Early Doubts and Skepticism

Despite widespread acceptance, some scientists expressed skepticism. The prominent anatomist David Waterston and the American zoologist Gerrit Smith Miller both questioned the validity of the fossils as early as 1913. They argued that the skull and jawbone did not belong to the same creature—the skull was human, and the jawbone was from an ape, possibly an orangutan.

Their critiques, however, were largely overshadowed by the prevailing enthusiasm. The scientific community, eager for discoveries that confirmed existing theories, dismissed these doubts. The allure of the Piltdown Man was too great, and the evidence seemed too compelling to refute.

The Unraveling Begins

The Piltdown Man remained a cornerstone of paleoanthropology until after World War II. Advances in dating methods and new fossil discoveries elsewhere began to cast doubt on the Piltdown fossils' authenticity. In Africa and Asia, hominid fossils were unearthed that presented a different evolutionary path—one that did not align with the features of the Piltdown Man.

In 1949, Kenneth Oakley of the British Museum applied a new fluorine absorption test to the Piltdown fossils. This method estimated the age of bones based on their fluoride content. The results were shocking: the Piltdown fossils were much younger than claimed. The skull and jawbone had significantly different fluorine levels, suggesting they were not from the same period.

Further analyses using nitrogen content tests and radiocarbon dating confirmed these discrepancies. The skull was determined to be medieval in origin, about 600 years old, while the jawbone was even more recent.

Exposing the Hoax

In 1953, a team comprising Kenneth Oakley, physical anthropologist Joseph Weiner, and anatomist Wilfrid Le Gros Clark conducted a thorough investigation. They revealed that the Piltdown fossils had been deliberately altered. The bones had been stained with chemicals like potassium dichromate to appear older. The teeth showed file marks under microscopic examination, indicating they had been shaped to mimic human wear patterns.

The animal fossils and stone tools found at the site were also found to be from various locations and periods, planted to create a convincing prehistoric environment. The Piltdown Man was conclusively declared a forgery.

The Fallout and Reflection

The revelation sent shockwaves through the scientific community. How could such a deception have gone unnoticed for decades?

The Piltdown Man had influenced generations of research, leading scientists down a false path and hindering the understanding of human evolution.

The incident prompted a critical examination of scientific practices. It highlighted the dangers of bias, nationalism, and the uncritical acceptance of data that fits preconceived notions. The Piltdown hoax became a seminal case study of the importance of skepticism and rigorous verification in science.

Who Was the Culprit?

The identity of the forger remains one of the greatest mysteries in scientific history. Numerous individuals have been implicated over the years, but none have been definitively proven responsible.

Charles Dawson

As the primary discoverer, Dawson is a prime suspect. His reputation as an amateur archaeologist eager for recognition, combined with his involvement in other questionable findings, suggests a possible motive and means. Some believe he orchestrated the hoax to gain prestige within the scientific community.

Arthur Smith Woodward

Though a respected scientist, Woodward's unwavering support for the Piltdown Man, even in the face of mounting contradictory evidence, has raised suspicions. However, many argue that his credibility and lack of direct evidence against him make his involvement unlikely.

Pierre Teilhard de Chardin

The French Jesuit priest and paleontologist was present during some of the excavations and discovered a fossilized canine tooth at the site. Some suggest he participated in the hoax as a prank or philosophical statement. Yet, his esteemed career and lack of concrete evidence linking him to the forgery cast doubt on this theory.

Sir Arthur Conan Doyle

The creator of Sherlock Holmes lived near Piltdown and was acquainted with Dawson. Some speculate that he orchestrated the hoax as revenge against the scientific community for dismissing spiritualism, a belief he ardently supported. This theory, while intriguing, is largely considered speculative fiction.

The Lessons Learned

The Piltdown Man hoax serves as a powerful reminder of the importance of scientific integrity. It underscores how confirmation bias—the tendency to interpret new evidence as confirmation of one's existing beliefs—can lead even the most intelligent minds astray.

The incident also highlights the role of nationalism in science. The desire to place England at the center of human evolution may have clouded judgment, allowing the hoax to persist. It is a stark example of how cultural and personal biases can impede objective analysis.

The Impact on Paleoanthropology

Despite its negative aspects, the Piltdown episode ultimately strengthened scientific methodologies. It led to the development of more rigorous standards for evaluating fossil discoveries, including better dating techniques and interdisciplinary verification processes.

The exposure of the hoax accelerated the acceptance of the African origins of humanity, as suggested by the fossil records discovered by Raymond Dart and others. It cleared the way for a more accurate understanding of human evolution, unencumbered by the false narrative that had been perpetuated.

To this day, the full truth behind the Piltdown Man remains elusive. While Charles Dawson is the most likely perpetrator, definitive proof is lacking. Advances in forensic science have allowed for new investigations, including DNA analysis of the fossils and materials used in the forgery, but no conclusive answers have emerged.

The Piltdown Man continues to fascinate as a cautionary tale and a historical enigma. It challenges us to consider the ethical responsibilities of scientists and the vigilance required to guard against deception.

Reflecting on the Forbidden History

The Piltdown hoax is a prime example of how forbidden history can distort our understanding of the world. For over four decades, it misled scientists and the public alike, embedding falsehoods into the accepted narrative of human evolution. It demonstrates how easily history can be manipulated when evidence is fabricated or misinterpreted.

This incident urges us to critically examine the foundations of our knowledge and remain open to reevaluating long-held beliefs in light of new evidence. It also highlights the need for transparency and accountability in scientific research.

The story of the Piltdown Man is more than a tale of deception; it is a mirror reflecting the vulnerabilities of human nature—even within the disciplined realm of science. It reminds us that the pursuit of truth requires humility, skepticism, and a steadfast commitment to integrity.

Chapter 26: Unearthing the Veiled Legacy of Advanced Civilizations

Imagine a world where the narrative of human progress is drastically different from the one widely accepted today. A world where advanced civilizations thrived millions of years before the dawn of modern humans, leaving behind artifacts and evidence that challenge our fundamental understanding of history and evolution. This is not a work of fiction but a compilation of reports and discoveries that have been systematically overlooked, dismissed, or actively suppressed by the scientific community. Welcome to the forbidden history of our advanced culture—a history that, if acknowledged, will not only redefine our past but also reshape our perception of human potential.

The Mystery of Ancient Artifacts in Ancient Strata

The prevailing scientific consensus posits that human civilization began to flourish approximately 200,000 years ago, with the earliest known tools dating back to around 2.5 million years. Yet, numerous reports from the 19th and early 20th centuries describe artifacts and skeletal remains found in geological contexts that predate these timelines by millions of years. These findings are not mere anomalies but are indicative of a level of sophistication that contradicts established archaeological records.

1. Aix-en-Provence: Limestone Layers Concealing Ancient Mastery

In the late 18th century, French quarry workers near Aix-en-Provence unearthed fragments of what appeared to be meticulously carved stone columns embedded within deep limestone strata, approximately forty to fifty feet below the surface. Accompanying these remnants were coins, hammer handles, and wooden tool fragments, all suggesting an advanced level of craftsmanship. The presence of a board resembling masonry planks further implies organized construction activities far earlier than acknowledged.

2. Philadelphia's Marble Block: Inscriptions from the Depths

By 1830, a peculiar discovery emerged from a marble quarry near Philadelphia—a solid block containing letter-like shapes etched into the stone at depths of sixty to seventy feet. The precision of these characters indicates intentional human inscription, challenging the notion that such engravings emerged only with the rise of literate civilizations.

3. Scotland's Devonian Sandstone: Anachronistic Nails

The mid-19th century brought reports from Scotland's Kingoodie Quarry, where a nail was found embedded within Devonian sandstone, dating back approximately 360 to 408 million years. The nail's secure placement within the rock formation suggests it was not a result of post-quarrying activity, implying the presence of metalworking skills in an era long before humans are believed to have existed.

4. Precambrian Metalwork: Massachusetts' Mysterious Vessel

In 1852, workers in Dorchester, Massachusetts, discovered a metallic vessel within Precambrian pudding stone, estimated to be over 600 million years old. The vessel, adorned with intricate silver inlays, defies natural formation processes, indicating advanced metalworking capabilities incompatible with the geological age of the surrounding rock.

Geological Contexts and Their Implications

The artifacts mentioned above are not isolated incidents but are part of a broader pattern where human-made objects appear in geological layers that significantly predate the existence of Homo sapiens. This raises critical questions about the continuity and progression of human civilization:

- **Stratigraphic Integrity:** Many of these finds are reported from undisturbed geological strata, suggesting that the artifacts were not intrusive contaminants but genuine remnants from the time the layers were formed.
- **Technological Discrepancies:** The sophistication of the tools and artifacts often surpass that of known contemporaneous civilizations, indicating either a hidden lineage of advanced societies or the existence of lost technological milestones.

Challenges in Authentication and Acceptance

Despite the compelling nature of these discoveries, mainstream science has largely dismissed or ignored them due to several factors:

- **Source Credibility:** Many reports originate from non-scientific sources or are anecdotal, lacking rigorous documentation and peer-reviewed validation.
- **Preservation Bias:** Artifacts of extraordinary antiquity are rarely preserved in standard natural history museums, making verification and study difficult.
- **Scientific Preconceptions:** The entrenched belief in a linear progression of human evolution creates resistance to accepting evidence that contradicts established timelines and narratives.

Case Studies: Detailed Examination of Anomalous Finds

1. The Trenton Femur: A Modern Limb in Ancient Soil

In 1899, a human femur was discovered in Trenton, New Jersey, lying 91 inches beneath the surface within sediment layers dating back approximately 107,000 years. Despite being morphologically identical to modern human femurs, mainstream paleoanthropologists dismissed its antiquity, attributing its presence to recent intrusive burial or contamination.

2. Galley Hill Skeleton: Undisturbed Layers and Modern Anatomy

The Galley Hill site near London, England, revealed a human skeleton embedded in chalk strata approximately 330,000 years old. Witnesses, including geologist M. H. Heys, reported no signs of disturbance, supporting the hypothesis of an ancient human presence. However, subsequent scientific skepticism led to the skeleton's dismissal, primarily due to its modern anatomical features conflicting with the expected morphology of ancient humans.

3. Moulin Quignon Jaw: A Skeletal Puzzle in Miocene Strata

Discovered in 1863, the Moulin Quignon jaw in France was initially supported by a joint commission declaring its authenticity. Yet, scientific opinion shifted as the Neanderthal theory gained prominence, relegating the jaw to obscurity. Recent revelations suggest additional discoveries at the site that bolster the jaw's authenticity, challenging the dismissal based on evolutionary preconceptions.

4. Calaveras Skull: A Contested Relic from the Tertiary

The Calaveras Skull, found in California's gold mines in the 1860s, remains one of the most contentious artifacts. While some geologists and paleontologists affirm its authenticity and antiquity, others argue it is a modern intrusion or forgery. The skull's disappearance from museum records adds another layer of mystery, leaving its true origins unresolved.

The Suppression of Evidence: Institutional Barriers and Scientific Dogma

A recurring theme in these accounts is the systematic dismissal or suppression of evidence that challenges established scientific narratives. Factors contributing to this phenomenon include:

- **Scientific Conservatism:** The preference for theories with extensive support leads to the marginalization of unconventional findings.
- **Professional Rivalries:** Disputes among scientists and the desire to protect reputations can result in biased interpretations of evidence.
- **Lack of Documentation:** Many anomalous discoveries lack comprehensive records, making it easier for the scientific community to disregard them without thorough investigation.

The Call for Re-evaluation: Embracing Anomalous Evidence

To advance our understanding of human history, it is imperative to re-examine these anomalous findings with an open mind and rigorous scientific methodology. This involves:

- **Revisiting Original Sites:** Conducting new excavations and employing modern dating techniques to verify the context and age of artifacts and remains.
- **Cross-Disciplinary Collaboration:** Encouraging cooperation between archaeologists, geologists, paleontologists, and other relevant disciplines to ensure comprehensive analysis.
- **Challenging Preconceptions:** Recognizing and addressing inherent biases within the scientific community that may hinder the acceptance of groundbreaking evidence.

The evidence presented in this chapter underscores the necessity of questioning and potentially redefining the accepted timelines of human advancement. While mainstream science remains resistant to these challenges, the persistent nature of these anomalous discoveries suggests that there is more to uncover about our ancient past. Embracing these findings could illuminate hidden chapters of human history, revealing a legacy of sophistication and ingenuity that has long been concealed from the annals of accepted knowledge.

Chapter 27: Ape-Like Men and the Forbidden History of Africa

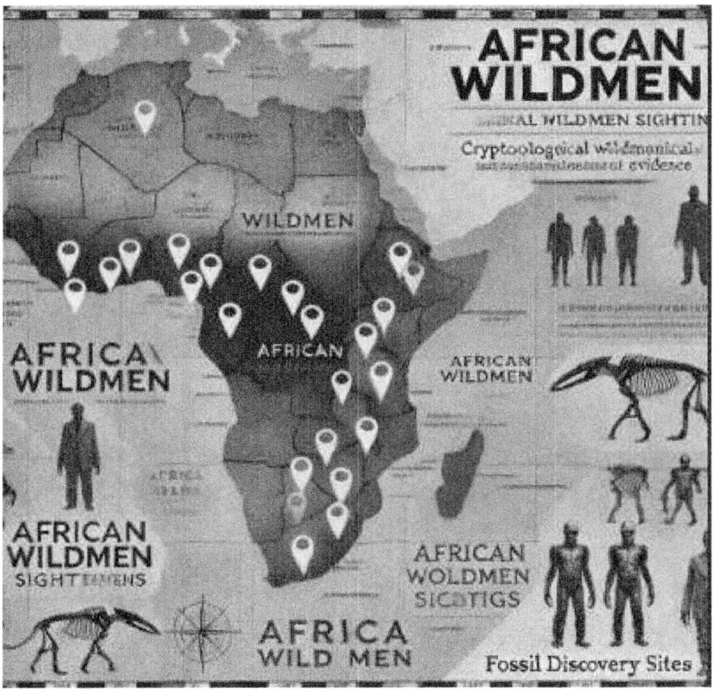

The narrative of human evolution, as dictated by mainstream science, presents a linear progression from primitive apelike ancestors to the sophisticated Homo sapiens we recognize today. However, beneath this polished facade lies a tumultuous history fraught with controversies, suppressed evidence, and deliberate obfuscations. This chapter delves into the clandestine realm of Africa's forbidden history, challenging the established paradigms and exposing the undeniable coexistence of modern humans with more primitive hominids.

The Limitations of Empirical Science

Empirical methods, while foundational to scientific inquiry, are not infallible. The fossil record, often hailed as the ultimate arbiter of our evolutionary past, is inherently incomplete and riddled with gaps. Fossilization is a rare event, susceptible to countless variables that can distort or erase evidence. This inherent imperfection means that our understanding of human ancestry is built on a fragile scaffold, easily toppled by new, contradicting evidence.

When scrutinized objectively, the accumulation of fossil evidence and contemporary reports of living apelike hominids paints a picture of coexistence rather than the neatly sequenced evolution posited by conventional science. This reality suggests a more complex and intertwined history of hominids, where multiple species may have thrived simultaneously across different regions.

Africa: The Cradle of Controversy

Africa, often revered as the cradle of humanity, is also the epicenter of some of the most perplexing and suppressed evidence challenging the mainstream evolutionary narrative. Reports from various regions within Africa recount encounters with wildmen—beings that defy classification and blur the lines between humans and apes.

Western Africa: The Agogwe and Kakundakari

In the western parts of Africa, particularly the Ivory Coast, indigenous informants describe encounters with pygmy-like creatures covered in reddish hair. European explorers corroborate these accounts, adding layers of credibility to the indigenous testimonies. Capt. William Kitchens, during a lion hunt in 1937 within the dense forests of Tanzania, witnessed two small, upright-walking, russet-haired beings disappearing into the thickets. These creatures, known locally as Agogwe, have been reported consistently across Tanzania and Mozambique.

Similarly, in the Congo region, legends speak of the Kakundakari and Kilomba—hominids standing over five and a half feet tall, covered in hair, and walking upright. Charles Cordier, an esteemed animal collector in the late 1950s and early 1960s, pursued tracks of the Kakundakari in Zaire. His accounts include a vivid description of a Kakundakari entangled in a bird snare, swiftly removing the noose and escaping before human intervention.

Southern Africa: From Tobias to Modern Skepticism

Pascal Tassy, a notable figure in vertebrate and human paleontology, recounts reports of wildmen from southern Africa. Philip V. Tobias, a respected authority on Australopithecus, once revealed that colleagues had set traps aiming to capture living australopithecines. These accounts are not relics of the past; sightings persist, suggesting that these apelike hominids might still roam Africa's remote wilderness.

Despite the abundance of eyewitness testimonies, mainstream anthropology, and zoology largely dismiss the existence of wildmen. Established scientists often sideline these reports, focusing instead on evidence that aligns with their preconceived notions of human evolution. This deliberate exclusion of contradictory evidence ensures the perpetuation of a singular, sanitized narrative of human ancestry.

The Fossil Evidence: Challenging the Evolutionary Timeline

Reck's Skeleton: A Puzzling Find

In 1913, Professor Hans Reck of Berlin University unearthed a skeleton at Olduvai Gorge in Tanzania, then part of German East Africa. Reck identified the skeleton as anatomically modern, dating it to approximately 1.15 million years ago based on its stratigraphic position in Bed II. However, this classification was met with immediate skepticism from contemporaries like Louis Leakey, who later revisited the site and questioned the skeleton's age.

The debate intensified when geologists Cooper and Watson suggested that the skeleton had been intrusively buried, contaminating the stratigraphic layers and rendering the initial dating invalid. Subsequent radiocarbon tests by Reiner Protsch in 1974 yielded a startlingly young date of 16,920 years. However, these results are widely regarded as unreliable due to potential contamination from preservative agents and environmental factors.

Despite Leakey's eventual concession that the skeleton might not belong to Bed II, the original claim of an anatomically modern human at such an ancient strata remains a thorn in the side of established paleoanthropological timelines. This discovery, along with others, suggests that modern humans or human-like beings might have existed far earlier than mainstream science acknowledges.

Kanam and Kanjera: The Shifting Sands of Hominid Classification

Louis Leakey's discoveries at Kanam and Kanjera further muddied the waters of human evolution. Initially hailed as evidence of Homo sapiens in the Early and Middle Pleistocene, these fossils exhibited a perplexing blend of modern and apelike features. The Kanam jaw, with its humanlike chin structure, and the Kanjera skulls, bearing both Homo sapiens and Neanderthal-like traits, defied easy classification.

Radiometric dating presented another layer of complexity. Fluorine and nitrogen content tests suggested that these humanlike fossils were contemporaneous with their faunal assemblages, implying an antiquity that contradicts established timelines. Uranium content analyses hinted at a younger age, yet these results were inconclusive and potentially flawed due to environmental variations.

The inability to definitively classify these fossils undermines the rigid framework of human evolution, indicating that multiple hominid species may have coexisted, each with varying degrees of humanlike and apelike characteristics.

Australopithecus and Homo habilis: The Fractured Lineage

Australopithecus, once celebrated as a direct ancestor of Homo sapiens, has come under intense scrutiny. Early reconstructions depicted Australopithecus as a bipedal hominid with a combination of humanlike and apelike features. However, subsequent analyses by anthropologists like Charles E. Oxnard and Bernard Heuvelmans have debunked this portrayal, arguing that Australopithecus exhibits a mosaic of traits that do not neatly align with either modern humans or apes.

Homo habilis, initially classified as a direct descendant of Australopithecus with enhanced tool-making capabilities, has also been destabilized. The discovery of OH 62, a Homo habilis skeleton with a diminutive stature and apelike limbs, contradicts earlier depictions of this species as a humanlike toolmaker. Furthermore, the association of Homo habilis with fossils exhibiting significant variation in morphology suggests a potential conflation of multiple species under a single taxonomic label.

These inconsistencies expose the fragility of the established human evolutionary tree, revealing that what was once considered a clear lineage is, in fact, a tangled web of overlapping species and shared characteristics.

Mainstream Science: Silencing the Evidence

Despite mounting evidence supporting the coexistence of modern humans with apelike hominids, mainstream science remains obstinately silent. Prominent anthropologists and zoologists dismiss wildman reports as folklore or misidentifications, while simultaneously ignoring substantial fossil evidence that challenges their assertions.

The operation of a "knowledge filter" ensures that any data undermining the established narrative is relegated to the fringes of scientific discourse, never to infiltrate the hallowed halls of museums or academic institutions. This systematic suppression of inconvenient truths serves to maintain the integrity of the conventional evolutionary timeline, regardless of the burgeoning evidence to the contrary.

However, a handful of reputable scientists, including Grover S. Krantz, John R. Napier, Myra Shackley, and Boris Porshnev, have dared to challenge the status quo. Their rigorous analyses and unwavering commitment to uncovering the truth lend credence to the existence of wildmen and the possibility of a more complex evolutionary history than previously acknowledged.

The Legacy of Suppressed Discoveries

The saga of African hominid discoveries is emblematic of the broader struggles faced by researchers challenging entrenched scientific paradigms. From Reck's contentious skeleton to the enigmatic Kanam jaw and the elusive Homo habilis, each discovery serves as a testament to the convoluted and often obstructed path toward unraveling our true origins.

The persistent existence of wildmen reports across diverse African regions, coupled with fossil evidence that defies simplistic classification, underscores the necessity for a paradigm shift in our understanding of human evolution. Ignoring or dismissing this evidence not only stifles scientific progress but also perpetuates a distorted view of our ancestral past.

To truly comprehend the depth and breadth of human evolution, the scientific community must confront the inconvenient truths presented by wildmen reports and anomalous fossil discoveries. This entails a departure from rigid, linear models of evolution towards a more nuanced and interconnected framework that accommodates the coexistence of multiple hominid species.

Conclusion: The Importance of Forbidden History

In concluding your book, "Forbidden History," we are reminded of the mysteries, the ignored evidence, and the suppressed truths that pervade human history. Through each chapter, we have explored the profound gaps in mainstream narratives—challenging the very foundations of what we've been taught about our origins, beliefs, and the hidden influences that shape our world. From the enigma of early human evolution to the lost wisdom of ancient civilizations, the veiled knowledge of secret societies, and the controversial realms of attraction and sexuality, each page has peeled back layers of the unknown.

Our journey has shown that history is not merely a linear account but a tapestry woven with threads of complexity, wonder, and hidden agendas. As we've traversed these forbidden histories, we've encountered artifacts, texts, and cultures that defy explanation—artifacts buried in time, suppressed by institutions and ignored by scientific orthodoxy. These discoveries compel us to question: who controls the story of humanity? Why has so much been kept from us, and what is the cost of ignorance?

Yet, this is not only a revelation of hidden truths but a call to action. Just as we've ventured into the forbidden, so too must future generations dig deeper, ask tougher questions, and dare to confront the structures that seek to confine knowledge. Our exploration is far from over. While mainstream narratives may offer comfort, the real story of humanity lies in the questions we continue to ask. With open minds and relentless curiosity, we pave the way for a deeper understanding of our place in the cosmos.

This book does not provide all the answers, but it illuminates a path—a journey beyond the limits of accepted history. It invites you, the reader, to continue seeking, to remain curious, and to embrace the adventure of questioning the forbidden. For in the pursuit of truth, we find not only knowledge but the very essence of what it means to be human.

Printed in Great Britain
by Amazon

55643906R00165